Turning Your Teen Around

How a couple helped their troubled son — while keeping their marriage alive and well

Betsy Tice White

Recovery Communications, Inc.
P.O. Box 19910 • Baltimore, Maryland 21211 • (410) 243-8558

For

My mother
who knew the healing power of God and A.A.

My father
who taught me to endure

My brother
the first addict I ever cared about

My husband and children
for their loyalty and love

The information presented herein is not intended to be considered counseling or other professional advice by the publisher, author, or contributors.

Book design by Belle Vista Graphics

Library of Congress Catalog Card Number: 96-067290
International Standard Book Number: 0-9615995-5-3

Contents

Special Sections:

Chapter One

A Good Family And A Problem Kid

When it started, he was only 12 years old.

How I looked forward to becoming a teen-ager! That magical age is an eagerly awaited milestone for everyone. Yet a dark cloud shadowed my growing-up years, because I had a half-brother twenty years my senior who was an alcoholic. That absent brother's influence was as pervasive and as powerful as if he were right there in our house.

Our dad felt ashamed and guilty for the way his son had turned out and tried to control Brother's actions through disapproval, rescuing, and money-manipulation. My mother, who loved her stepson, saw that Dad's strategy didn't work, but she was overruled. And as the only child at home, I was caught in the middle.

I remember a breezy, sunny Saturday in our small-town neighborhood full of kids. The younger children were playing Kick-the-Can in the street, while the older boys braved the giant swing in the big elm. Only one little girl was missing from the crowd. My parents were quarreling about Brother's latest escapade, and I had gone up to my room and shut the door, pulled down the shade, and turned on my little copper bedside lamp.

People said I was a pretty child. Wearing glasses, with my brown hair in braids, that day I had on my favorite plaid skirt and green sweater with a design of Scottie dogs, my saddle oxfords, and white ankle socks. The other children's playful cries left me feeling lonely, sad, and empty inside. The idea of venturing out into their rough-and-tumble play terrified me. I couldn't stand being knocked down onto the prickly grass to smother under a pile of arms and legs. The very idea made me feel sick at my stomach, made my palms sweat, my legs weak.

So instead of going out to play, I drew a careful plan and

5

methodically rearranged my bed, my desk and chair, my small bookcase with its books, and that cozy little lamp. I had discovered that within my own room, at least, I could overcome the scary unpredictability of our home. By bringing order and warmth to my own space, I could momentarily soothe myself, surrounding myself with a shell of security. By closing my door, I could shut all the unhappiness out.

I pulled out a favorite book about Raggedy Ann and Raggedy Andy and the Deep, Deep Woods and curled up on my bed in the corner. I smiled as I read, grateful for my soft pillow, my familiar quilt Grandma had made especially for me, and the warmth shed by my little lamp.

In that plain, small room, I had learned to create a controlled, precious, comforting sense of stability that lasted until one of my parents called.

Later, as my teen friends chattered away about boys, dates, and dances, I relayed messages between my parents when they weren't speaking to each other. On a frosty Friday after Dad picked me up from a high-school football game, I had to wait in the car chewing my fingernails to the quick while Dad plodded inside Brother's house to patch up after another domestic brawl.

Where money was concerned, I had to seek a college scholarship because so much money had gone to feed Brother's family and rescue Brother from the consequences of his binges. I thought I was the only teen-ager forced to live under such a cloud. Today, I know that I was far from alone.

Growing up prematurely burdened as my parents agonized over an addicted son, I resolved that, with my future life's partner, I would create a haven of harmony where my own children could grow up happy and free.

After I had become a wife and mother, Dad phoned one day with heart-breaking news. Brother was dead, of a combination of whiskey and prescription drugs. I grieved deeply for that beloved brother who never got well. Dad grieved even more. Tragedy having dashed all hopes for his only son, he himself lived just two years more.

My own generation must come to terms today with an even more terrible reality: a third of all teen-agers have serious problems with alcohol and other drugs. Young people flock to rock concerts where drug-taking is virtually universal. Parents who leave town return to find their home trashed. Alcohol-related highway accidents are a leading cause of teen deaths. Adolescent suicide is at an all-time high, and most young corpses contain alcohol, other drugs, or both. No wonder we parents are scared for our kids.

My husband Bob and I knew none of these facts. We simply worked hard at being good parents. We took our youngsters — Susan, John, and Mike — to Sunday school, church groups, Scouts, and every other place where moral values were upheld and responsible living taught.

To eliminate the lure of the forbidden, we accepted alcohol in moderation in our home and social life. At dinner we sometimes allowed our children sips of beer or wine. We assumed they would thus learn to use alcohol responsibly, forgetting that providing alcohol to a minor is absolutely against the law.

As our kids grew, Bob took the boys fishing and hunting. I taught all three children to cook and enjoyed their help in the kitchen. We went on hikes and picnics. When I took a job, I arranged to be home for that important after-school time with my kids. Bob's medical specialty practice allowed him to be home most nights and weekends.

In the early years, our three seemed model children — bright, lively, good-natured. They did well in school and behaved as well as others their age. They took an active part in church life and had plenty of friends. Until our John's twelfth birthday, he was a well-behaved honor-roll student with many hobbies: magic tricks, model building, coin and stamp collecting. He loved to read and played a five-string banjo extremely well.

When a soccer league was formed, both John and 10-year-old Mike joined. The plan was that they would practice twice a week after school; I always picked them up on my way home. But one afternoon when I drove up to the soccer field Mike waited alone.

"Mike, where's John?"

"He told Coach he had to leave early and went to Stu Sutton's house. Are you gonna punish him?"

"I don't know. We'll see. Mrs. Sutton teaches school, so she's probably not home." I drove to the Suttons'. John and Stu were there; Mrs. Sutton was not. I told John to get in the car. "Son, you must stay at soccer practice until I come."

"Okay," John said.

I told Mrs. Sutton what had happened, then forgot about it. A week later the same thing happened again. This time Bob and I agreed to ground John for a week, believing we had the problem solved.

A month later as I pulled up beside the playing field, I spotted John and Stu coming through the hedge at the far end. Again Mike spilled the beans. "John never stays at practice any more. He leaves with Stu before Coach gets here. They come back just before you pick us up."

"Michael, why didn't you tell me this before?

"John said he'd beat me up."

"Does he leave every time?"

"Every time."

My boy had been successfully deceiving me for weeks. As I watched him walk toward me, my temples throbbed and my stomach cramped. Resisting the frightening fact that I was losing control of a 12-year-old, I gripped the steering wheel so tightly that my knuckles turned white.

After John got in the car neither of us said a word. I just drove the car automatically, preoccupied with worries and fears. At home I pulled into the garage with a jerk, got out and slammed the car door, and marched grimly inside.

Worried, disappointed, and confused, I went to my room and threw myself on the bed. My heart was pounding; my knees felt weak. Curled in a ball, I clenched and unclenched my fists, trying to steady my breathing and slow my heart.

I longed to escape into a deep, deep sleep — just close my eyes, settle down under the warm comforter, and leave everything behind!

Outside, the trees were putting on the multi-colored tapestry that means fall, yet their glory went unnoticed by me. Boys' voices drifted in from the basketball goal in the drive. I would have to keep tabs on what they were about. Getting up, I looked back longingly at that peaceful bed. It would have felt so good to stay there forever if I could.

After Bob came home we concluded that the previous punishment had been too light. This time we grounded our older boy for an entire month. Thereafter on soccer days I left work early and sat in my car at the athletic field for an hour, to make sure that John didn't leave.

My child's misbehavior had begun to alter my own life.

In the weeks that followed, John became a problem child, misbehaving repeatedly. We lectured, grounded him, stopped his allowance, trying to maintain control of this suddenly wayward boy. Conflicts in our household increased. At the slightest provocation from 16-year-old Susie or Mike, John shouted, shoved, scratched, and pummeled them. Bob or I always stepped in to keep the peace.

Worrisome phone calls came from John's teachers and then the principal. Every few days it was something new. John was punished both at school and at home, but his behavior did not change.

When John came home with an assignment to complete at the university library, I gave him permission to go. Thereafter he asked to go back with classmates twice a week; I picked him up routinely at half past five.

And then one afternoon it got to be five forty-five, then six o'clock. I was getting worried when a uniformed officer came up to my car.

"Excuse me, ma'am, are you Mrs. White?"

"Yes, is anything wrong?"

"Follow me over to Campus Security, please. We have your son and another boy in custody. The chief wants to see all the parents right away."

I turned the key in the ignition, hands sweating, heart racing. As the patrol car passed I spotted John in the back seat, obviously feeling trapped and sick. Beside him cowered his friend Brett, looking much the same.

I followed the patrol car through the campus, my fear and anger mingled with shame. Why was John causing so much trouble? Why couldn't he be a "good" boy like everyone else's child?

Chapter ↪ Two

Probation, Pot, And Putting Up With "This Stuff"

Our pre-teen had us all in his control.

John and Brett waited in the hall while I followed the officer back to Chief Martin's desk. "Please sit down, Mrs. White," the security chief said. "Several weeks ago we began finding photocopies of dollar bills in the campus change machines." He held one out for me to see. "Somebody was putting these in and getting quarters back — several hundred dollars a week. The city police found the same thing at a car wash. We set up a stake-out. These two boys showed up and started feeding in fake bills."

I swallowed hard. "What happens next?"

"John's dad and Brett's parents need to come. We've called in the U.S. Treasury agent. You'll have to wait here until he comes."

Why is all this happening to me? I thought as I dialed our home number, told Bob briefly about the trouble, then sat down to wait. What were we going to do with this boy?

All the things John had brought home lately — T-shirts, record albums, a digital watch — had been bought with money he had stolen all over town.

Brett's mom and dad came; soon afterward Bob walked in. The four of us waited in sick silence for two long hours.

The Treasury agent finally arrived. "What we're dealing with here is a violation of Federal law," he said. "John and Brett, you've been counterfeiting U.S. currency."

I could hear the cellblock door clanging shut. The agent went on. "Federal law makes no distinction between adult and juvenile crime, but I'm not interested in sending twelve-year-olds to Federal prison. I have teen-age youngsters myself, and I think you boys deserve a chance to straighten up before you get into worse trouble. I'm here to convince you that the Federal law is very serious business."

He paused so his words could sink in. "We're asking the city's juvenile court system to take over this case. That will satisfy the Federal authorities and possibly serve everyone's good." My relief was so great, I could barely hold back my tears.

Within weeks John and Brett sat in a courtroom along with four sad and embarrassed parents. The judge heard the facts, then asked the fathers to speak.

"Your honor," said Bob when his turn came, "John's mother and I have decided — if you approve — to enroll John in boarding school when he turns thirteen. We believe a strict environment will straighten him out."

"Reasonable enough," said the judge. "I'm giving these boys one more chance. But if they violate their year's probation or commit a second offence, there'll be no further chance."

I walked out of the courthouse burdened with an invisible load of guilt and shame. Surely this was Bob's and my fault — didn't bad parents make bad kids?

Thereafter, in the hallway at work, I kept my gaze focused on my feet. In the cafeteria I chose an out-of-the-way table and spread my dishes out so no one would join me or expect me to make normal conversation. My work suffered; my thoughts kept straying to my wayward son.

My body suffered, too. A pain in my lower left abdomen never went away. My neck and shoulders were chronically sore, and by late afternoon I always had a tension headache that wouldn't quit. The ordinary pleasures of life escaped me. Sex became routine or an infrequent duty, which didn't help the relationship between Bob and me.

What got me through those troubling days? To begin with, just putting one foot in front of the other. When I woke in the morning, dead tired, the smell of coffee made early by Bob got me out of bed. My shower's warmth got me ready to dress. The second cup of coffee and sausage biscuit I picked up on the way to work got me across town.

Prayer helped. Every day I prayed, "Help me, God. Please change my son." When I dropped by our church between services just to sit quietly and repeat my prayer, the red sanctuary flame was a comfort, recalling that long-ago little copper lamp.

My two greatest comforts, however, came in the late-night hours: escape reading and big bowls of chocolate ice cream. My family knew about my murder mysteries, but that ice cream was a deep, dark secret. Even though eating it made me feel better for an hour or so, I was ashamed of turning to gluttony to ease my distress.

Bob and I were eager to get John into the boarding school for the next year. Our discipline wasn't working; perhaps someone else's would. We thought a change of scenery would do the trick, not knowing that the problem lay within John himself. In the addiction world, a change of environment is known as "the geographic cure," and it never works.

The boys' probation agreement called for summer jobs. John went to work on a farm and saved all his earnings for restitution. He behaved pretty well, but we feared that he might "go off" again at any time. I could hardly wait for him to be safely installed under a stern head-master's eye.

And so John left home at age thirteen. I sometimes lay awake at night after that, troubled by misgivings. Was he too young to fend for himself? I relied upon the assumption that we had placed him in the care of professional educators who knew what to do with boys like him.

At Thanksgiving John came home clearly troubled. He was rest-less, irritable, and depressed. Susie picked up on it immediately. After our Thanksgiving feast, once we had washed and dried the silver, china, and crystal and put everything away, we gathered around a cozy hearthfire in our family room, and Bob began to question John.

"Son, do you get along with your roommate?"

"I hate him! He's a rich snob, and he hates me too."

"Why do you say he hates you?"

"He makes fun of my clothes, my music, everything about me. In fact, everybody there treats me like dirt."

"What about your counselor?" asked Susie. "I bet he would help you work it out."

John was on the verge of tears. "He can't help. They all say I'm a weirdo! They call me the school freak!"

His pain was certainly real. Mike listened sympathetically. We continued to question but made no headway. Finally Bob went off to bed, while Susan and I sat up until two in the morning with John. All we got were pleas that he be allowed to come home.

"I'll do anything, anything you say," John begged.

"Mom, please beg Daddy to let John come back home," Susie said. "I don't believe he's making all this up."

Next morning I tackled Bob before the kids were up. "How would you feel about letting John come home?"

"What? Have you forgotten how it was before he left? I'm not ready to take all that on again."

"But, honey, he promises to do everything we tell him, if we'll just let him come back. The boy seems so miserable."

"I'll think about it," Bob said.

John soon had the three of us heavily involved in his campaign. Tender-hearted Susan wrote home from college to plead. Brother Mike said staunchly, "If you wouldn't let me come home, I'd run away!" I put in my own timely word.

By Christmas Bob finally softened. "I've made my decision, John. If you finish out the year and do well, you can come home to finish high school here — provided you do every single thing we expect of you."

John let out a whoop of joy and gave his dad a mammoth hug. "You won't be sorry, Dad!"

I felt like hugging my husband, all three kids, and even the dog. Keeping everyone happy was my self-appointed role, and I worked hard at it. The moments when I succeeded were among the few times that I could feel "all right."

Money problems plagued John all that year. Always short of funds, he declared that someone was stealing his money. Grumbling, Bob sent checks to make up the losses.

There was a logical reason why John was always out of cash: he had begun drinking and getting high on pot. After some upperclassmen introduced him to these drugs, he discovered that marijuana and alcohol relieved his loneliness and hurt, and he used them regularly thereafter. At Thanksgiving John may have been trying to ask for help. If so, it went unrecognized. We weren't mind-readers. John was already in bondage to his secret.

With summer, our boy came happily home to stay. He completed his probation and went back to the farm. I took him to the bank to open a checking account. Not knowing that a co-signature could be required, I gave my 14-year-old enough rope, figuratively speaking,

13

to hang himself. When his first bank statement came in, we had a battle royal. His balance was barely above zero. "You're making good money, son. Where's it all going?"

"It's my money, Mom," he snapped. "I worked for it, and I can do anything I want to with it. Quit hassling me!"

"We want you to learn to manage your money."

"Why don't you get off my back?" he exploded.

"If you mess up, I'm responsible."

"Okay, dammit! I just won't have a bank account." John stormed up to his room and slammed the door. This nasty scene was repeated a month later, with John even more hostile. He had written checks to "Cash" for $60 and $70.

Something was very wrong. I didn't know how to set things right, and I was afraid to try. My son's and my relationship had reached a new low. He had come close to destroying my self-confidence, my self-esteem.

Our family life went from tense to chaotic. John's moods became more erratic: one moment laughing and joking, an hour later sullen and withdrawn. We avoided anything that might rub him the wrong way. Even so, some things did provoke him, and he would then stomp upstairs, slam the door of his room, and lock it behind him.

When our boy's unpredictable moods and isolation became a pattern, I stopped fighting it and just totally adapted to this unhealthy way of life. Our entire household began to adapt to his craziness — we all believed this was the way things had to be. We knew of no other way to survive.

Yet John could be so nice when he chose! He kept us alternating between hope and despair, frustration and resolve. Riding that emotional roller-coaster was exhausting. We didn't know how to get off.

Equally exhausting were our efforts to keep track of John's whereabouts. We told him repeatedly to let us know exactly where he was going each time he left the house.

"No problem!" he would answer cheerfully, on his way out the door. "Call you when I get there!" But he never called, and now John was a free agent, walking all over town, hitchhiking, catching rides with friends. Trying to tighten up on him was like trying to lasso an eel.

With autumn, John returned to public high school. He got by

with a minimum of study and stretched out evenings on his bed with his stereo headphones. He began smoking tobacco in his room. We couldn't find a way to stop it; our bribes and punishments had no effect.

Bob and I drew on the latest books on bringing up teenagers. They told us: "The teen years are hard." "Be patient." "Kids have to rebel as part of growing up." "Teens need time to themselves." "It's important to respect a youngster's privacy." We followed the so-called experts' advice. But if these were the experts, why were we getting such bad results?

Mike knew why John was behaving in such bewildering ways, but he kept it to himself, for John had introduced Mike to the pleasures of pot smoking, exacting a pledge of silence. Mike, too, began to withdraw somewhat from the family circle, keeping the secret well.

My husband and I tried to pretend that neither our pain nor our problem existed. We gave up talking about our son. If we tried to talk to John, he came back with, "You're crazy! There's nothing wrong with me! If you'd get off my back, everything would be fine."

We began to think we might be crazy and John might be fine. We were firmly locked into denial.

We believed we would just have to try harder to understand our boy. The possibility that John might be an alcoholic or a drug addict at the age of fourteen was too horrible to endure.

Chapter Three

Cars, Wrecks, Guns

The courts, our pastor, John — all left me feeling crazy and like a parental failure.

John was painfully callous toward Mike. He rejected, ridiculed, fought, or ignored him, except when Mike had something he wanted — such as money. Mike knew that much of what John was doing was wrong, yet he wanted so much to be accepted by his big brother — a tough spot for a little kid.

When Susan went back to college, she remarked, "This family is always in an uproar on account of John. I know I should love him because he's my brother, but sometimes I almost hate him. He's turned into a real jerk. When I'm at school I don't have to worry about him, and it feels good."

I often felt like walking out myself, just leaving the misery behind. The peaceful framed seaside painting over our fireplace mantel, our shelves filled with familiar books, elegant draperies with their soft fringe, deep soft carpets, and lovely antiques — could I turn my back on all that for good?

My deep feelings for my husband, Bob, and my comfortable home kept me nailed down. I had enjoyed making those rooms pretty, searching out beautiful fabrics and the right piece of porcelain for that corner shelf. I treasured the antiques inherited from my family and the other nice things I had collected over the years. My Oriental rugs, my Sheraton desk, my baby grand piano told me who I was and where I came from, that I mattered, and that life could be very good. I couldn't leave all this behind.

Yet the most powerful magnet of all was my compulsion to rescue John from the consequences of his self-destructive acts. I couldn't walk out until that great day when John's problems were solved. But would that day ever come?

I threw myself into my job and tried to forget about things at home. The best spirit-lifter for me at work was a new co-worker, Lynne, a natural-born comedienne who sat at the desk across from mine. Worn out with the pain in my belly, my headaches, and always feeling sad, I found myself laughing heartily at Lynne during our coffee breaks and lunch hours. Her jokes and fun truly lightened those burdensome days.

Our best laugh came when a flighty divorcée in our department, who was always bragging about her male conquests, complained that she had lost her diaphragm. "Did you put an ad in the paper?" Lynne asked, all innocence. Joining in the general hilarity that followed felt so good!

But in spite of Lynne's antics, the office telephone kept bringing me back to reality — calls from the school, from other parents, from John himself, asking to leave school on various pretexts.

Bob found his own escape — competitive running — guaranteed to keep him away from home for hours at a time.

On John's fifteenth birthday he was up before the sun. "Who's going with me to get my learner's permit?" he demanded. Bob got up wearily and went with him to take the test. Even with permit in hand, John was a terrible driver — erratic, jumpy, unpredictable. Bob counted on time and training to remedy the situation. Any correction met with John's impatient scorn: "I know what I'm doing! For crying out loud, why can't you give me a chance?"

Confused and demoralized, neither of us could say no. John was absolutely in charge. Bob and I had completely lost touch with our parental backbone.

In the passenger seat Bob grew testier and testier, while Mike and I cowered in the back, praying to make it to our destination in one piece.

John's driving was just one of many situations in which we were unable to distinguish between the expected turmoil of adolescence and a drug-disordered nervous system. Normal adolescence naturally includes emotional ups and downs; not all such behavior is drug-induced. But when a progressive pattern includes isolation from the family, skipping school, dishonesty, emotional instability, conflict with everyone in the household, and loss of interest in former

17

activities and hobbies, it's a strong indication that a child is drinking, drugging, or both. Failing grades and disappearance of money or other valuables are further clues.

Parents who recognize these patterns must get help as soon as possible from support groups such as Families Anonymous, Narcotics Anonymous, or Al-Anon, and if possible from knowledgeable addictions professionals as well.

The sooner a family intervenes, the better the chances are that a drinking or drugging youngster can learn to live productively again. Delay will only make matters worse and could be fatal.

We needed help, but we didn't know how much. Nor did we know where to turn. We were keeping our problems locked up in our carefully constructed defenses of secrecy and guilt. We couldn't reveal our problems, for then everyone would think we had been parental failures — or so we believed.

During those worried weeks, "Pachelbel's Canon" hit the top of the pop-music charts. What a relief from John's heavy-metal rock! This tranquil little gem became my sure-fire channel of peace. I listened to my Pachelbel tape whenever I could, and for a brief moment there was beauty in my world again.

The beer joints in the nearby university town compounded our troubles. Buying alcohol was no problem for John or his underage friends. I found a fake I.D. card in John's wallet, cut it in pieces, and threw it away. He simply ordered another one from a comic book, the same way he had obtained the first.

Weekends were the roughest. Sometimes I stayed home, grinding my guts and worrying, alienated and lonely in the midst of my family crowd. I cried a lot, even when it wasn't appropriate to cry. I nearly wore out my knees praying: "Help me, God. Please change my son."

Occasionally I got braver, told my husband I needed a break, and headed out with my friend Isabel to visit every antique shop within miles. Isabel didn't know about our troubles at home; she just shared my love of antiques. Buying was not my object on those trips. Just getting away was one

of the few ways I could turn off the fear-and-worry tapes that
constantly played in my head.

I finally faced up to the possibility that John might also be using drugs and began to search his room. I came across some curious things: a dented beer can with holes punched in its top and side and what looked like a miniature tobacco pipe. John had explanations for both, leaving me feeling even more confused, guilty, and afraid. (The beer can was a homemade pot pipe. John bought the little ready-made pipe when the beer-can model failed to meet his needs.)

When I found rolling-papers in John's pocket, he said they belonged to a friend. When I asked about a bottle of eyedrops, he stormed, "What are you snooping around in my room for? They're normal eyedrops, the kind everybody uses."

The round mesh screens disappeared out of the faucet aerators (perfect for the bowl of his little pipe). A surgical clamp vanished from Bob's medical bag (a holder to permit smoking a joint down to the last nub). Tranquilizers disappeared from the bathroom medicine cabinet — we suspected the plumber! These things happened far enough apart that we never put it all together to complete the big picture. The previous mystery was forgotten by the time the next one cropped up.

All the signs were there; it was like the pictures in children's magazines, where you look for the Indian hidden in the tree limbs, or the hammer among the lily pads.

We could make no sense of our picture, because John was still doing many of the right things. He went to church with us regularly, took part in youth group, served as an altar boy. He made honor roll and got elected vice-president of his class. None of these things fit our imagined profile of an addict.

One Saturday in hunting season, John and Mike went to the woods to try for squirrels. We heard no shooting, and when they came home they were silly and giggling, their eyes fiery red.

"What's wrong with your eyes, boys?"

"Nothing," they said, finding my question hilarious.

Was I going crazy? Something was wrong. I went up to my room and closed the door, feeling sad, disturbed, shut out by these two under-age louts. Lying on my bed, I tried to figure out what was amiss, but I still didn't get it. Instead, I worried about their guns.

All the neighboring farm boys had guns and regularly hunted doves, rabbits, and squirrels. When I told Bob I was opposed to our boys having weapons, Bob said, "Oh, now, boys just naturally want to fool with guns. I'm teaching them the safe way to handle firearms, since they're going to do it anyway." He joined a gun club and enrolled our two in a hunting safety course.

My doubts hung on. "I still don't like the idea of having guns around. I worry about the boys getting hurt or hurting somebody else."

John and Mike had their stock answer: "Aw, Mom, you're so overprotective!" After being told that several hundred times, you can get to believe it. I finally gave up, leaving the matter of the guns to Bob.

One weekend I was in the kitchen and Bob was working in the garage, while John was up in his room behind that closed door. John came downstairs just as Bob entered the kitchen.

"John, you were supposed to wash the car today," Bob said.

"I'll do it after a while."

"Do it now. Get busy."

"I'll do it when I get ready," John muttered.

"Dammit, John, I want it done now!"

"You go to hell!" John exploded. He stormed out of the kitchen and up to his room. In moments he was back, wearing his shell vest and carrying his double-barreled shotgun. He paused in the kitchen long enough to chamber two shells.

"John!" I cried. "What are you doing?"

"None of your damn business," he snarled, elbowing past me and out the door toward the woods.

"Stop him, Bob! He mustn't have the gun when he's in that state!"

"I'm afraid to interfere. Didn't you see the rage in his face? He wouldn't hesitate to turn that gun on either of us!"

We could only stand by helplessly, waiting. The shooting began. John was firing as fast as he could reload — two explosions, a moment of quiet, then two more, on and on. We didn't know whether he was shooting into the air, at trees, or gathering nerve to shoot himself. It was a blood-chilling wait.

At last he ran out of ammunition and came back to the house, sullen, silent, his rage temporarily spent. We were afraid to speak. And John retreated once more behind that closed door.

After the shock wore off, I burst out of the house and ran to the woods, crying. I was shaking all over; my legs were wobbly, and I was afraid I might faint. When I came to a stump, I sank down unsteadily, hugging myself, begging for God's help. My knees were trembling. Even my teeth were chattering with the shock, but my prayer came out anyway — the same words I had prayed so many times: "Help me, God. Please change my son."

And this time as I prayed, a remarkable warmth grew within my breast, bringing with it the certainty that God's love was all around me, at that very moment, as it had always been, no matter how deep my pain. That certainty was larger than the trees, larger than the sky, larger than the world.

I just sat there in the woods with my tears dropping down, letting God love me. I knew that God cared for me, for all my family including John, and that a marvelous force was available to help us heal, if we opened ourselves to its power and love. By the time I returned to the house my legs were steady again, my breathing easy and slow. Most wonderful of all, my fear was gone.

Many days after that I returned to that same spot, hearing the wind in the branches, breathing the pine-tree fragrance, and remembering the assurance of the great love that had come to me there. I knew I could trust in that love to bring us through.

On Monday after the boys left for school, Bob carried all the guns to a friend's house for safekeeping. Even so, we lived constantly with the fear that John, enraged or despairing, might take his own life. Once he even told me so: "Mom, sometimes I'm afraid I might kill myself."

In my ignorance I turned it aside: "Son, don't even think of such a thing, much less talk about it." My response was a terribly risky one, because youngsters who express thoughts of suicide often go on to carry out the final deed, especially if drinking and drugging have made a mess of their lives. John could easily have killed himself on any of a number of occasions.

When John turned sixteen, after two tries he finally passed the driver's license test. In the first week that Bob let him take our car out on his own, he zoomed out of a filling station into a pickup truck. We made him pay for the damages, but our insurance premium soared.

John got busy and found himself a restaurant job so he could pay off the body shop. After his repair bill was paid, he bought an old car.

We raised no objection because we thought our own car would be spared. After that, he used both the car and his earnings as he pleased. His next wreck came on a weekend. High on pot and beer, John backed into the car of another youngster who was in the same shape. A passing policeman saw the accident and filed a report. Our insurance premium went up again just as we learned of this second mishap.

The third wreck came while John was driving to school. Another teen braked for a stoplight; John ran into her car from behind. During one year he laid out $1,800 for car repairs.

John was now staying out later and later on weekends, always with a plausible excuse. We believed him because we wanted to. The first night he stayed out past 2:00 A.M., I panicked. Bob had turned in early. I finally mustered the nerve to phone the parents of one of John's pals. An irritable male voice growled, "Who is it?"

"This is John's mother." I tried to sound casual. "Sorry to trouble you, but I'm a little worried about John. Is Chris home? I thought he might have some idea where John could be."

"Hold on, I'll ask." I waited. "Chris came in at twelve-thirty. He says the last he saw of John, he was down on Fifth Street, with Brett." That was the street where all the beer joints were.

I went through the same process with two other families. Nobody knew where John was. The telephone was slippery with my tears. At 3:45 John rolled in, knee-walking drunk. All he said to me was, "Shut up, bitch!" I watched him stagger upstairs, nursing my misery alone until daylight.

Next morning John was badly hung over, massively repentant. "Mom, Dad, I realize what a stupid thing I did last night. I feel rotten about it. I don't blame you for whatever you decide to do."

"You can hand over your car keys," Bob said. "You won't be driving any more this year."

"Yes, sir. I know I deserve it." John recognized that his behavior was out of line. He wanted to do better, and he tried. But the scene always ended in the same way. John went out. Bob went to bed. I waited up, going to the window a hundred times. Long past curfew John came dragging in, with slurred speech, red eyes, and unsteady gait. If I said anything, he either cursed me or stared me down in silent contempt.

Out of the twenty-four hours in a day, I became an expert on 3:00 A.M. I would lie in bed starkly awake, obsessing about John, thinking circular thoughts, tossing and turning, worrying

22

feverishly and soaking the pillow with my tears.

How did I make it through until daylight? Eventually I found a mind-game that helped. I would tell myself, "Hey, I'm doing this worrying stuff again tonight, when I'm too tired to find the solution. I'll try again tomorrow night, after I've had more rest." I actually reached a point of being able to turn over and go back to sleep!

Whenever I reported to Bob, I always tailored my story to protect John. I was shielding John from his father's anger and shielding my husband from the painful truth.

Crisis had become such a familiar state in our lives that I even began to savor my part in trying to keep the inferno under control!

Making myself responsible for everybody's actions, I was the operator at our family's emotional switchboard, receiving all the messages and feeling compelled to act on every one. And if there were any messages of importance for me, all the lines were so busy that my own "calls" couldn't get through.

When a family is struggling with addiction, everybody in that family begins to behave in crazy ways. Everybody in such a family needs and deserves help, the sooner the better.

Young Mike always stayed out of the line of fire. When a family conflict started warming up, he headed out to shoot baskets or turned up the volume on the TV. He knew a lot about John's habits that he wasn't telling — that John, drunk, got in a fistfight at a football game, which the police had to break up; or that while Bob and I were at a dinner party, John came in drunk again and vomited all over the bathroom before passing out. Mike cleaned up the mess, keeping the secret out of what seemed to him excellent motives — self-protection and loyalty. Like Bob and me, he failed to understand that John was slowly killing himself.

An addict? A drunk? Our boy was just sixteen! But John was both. Whenever he used alcohol or any other drug, the drug took over completely. He never knew whether he could drink one beer and stop, or go on to drink twenty and pass out. He never knew whether he could share a joint and call it quits, or smoke three more and swallow a handful of pills besides. No one, including John himself, could see what was happening. But by now it was beyond his power to stay sober or drug-free for more than a few days at a time. His chemicals had robbed him of the power to choose.

I felt sorry for myself, scared to death for my son, and altogether burned-out on life. Everyday existence hurt so bad, something had to change. On a day when I thought I couldn't stand it any longer, I went to see our pastor, hoping he could help. In tears, I poured out my troubles, telling him how much unhappiness my boys were causing me and that I didn't know what to do.

"All kids experiment with pot and beer," Father Lee said, echoing words we would hear from many others. "Be patient. They'll eventually grow up."

If my pastor had simply told me I needed a Families Anonymous, Al-Anon, or Nar-Anon meeting three times a week and offered to go with me himself, this book would be a lot shorter than it is.

He now knows to tell parishioners that, but back then he lacked the essential knowledge about addiction that would help.

Next, John's boss accused him of taking money out of the cash register. John flung down his apron. "You can forget about firing me," he said, "because I quit!" After that, he loafed around home for a month or two until he felt the pinch financially, then hustled up a new job as a busboy. The money was pretty good.

One day I came home from work earlier than usual to find John entertaining a visitor in our living room — a burly, bearded guy with an earring, wearing the standard black-leather motorcycle rig. He was making himself comfortable on my velvet-covered Chippendale couch, his oily boots sprawled out on my treasured Oriental rug.

"Mom, this is Angelo. Angelo, this is my mom," said John nervously. Who the deuce was Angelo, and what was this road warrior doing with my boy? I could tell Angelo was nervous in my presence; after he left, my first impulse was to check the dining-room sideboard to see if the family silver was still in place.

"John, who is Angelo, and what does he want with you?"

"You're so suspicious, Mom! He's the frycook at the restaurant. He's new in town and just wants some friends."

Thirty-year-old motorcycle buffs don't pal around with underage teens unless something very, very peculiar is going on. "That guy is bad news."

"Some Christian you are," John sneered. "Can't even be nice to a stranger in town."

"No, John! I don't want him around here ever!"
So John had to find other ways to see Angelo, for Angelo was a drug dealer, and John was one of his first local customers.

Springtime came — a bad time for families with drinking and drugging kids. One Saturday night John and three buddies chipped in for several six-packs and $10 worth of pot, consuming them in a downtown parking lot. The patrolman who arrested them walked the quartet straight to the city jail. For once John was home early, handing us his summons to appear in Municipal Court on a charge of unlawful possession of beer and marijuana.

Now we knew. John was using drugs, and he had graduated from juvenile court to the big boys' league.

Going to court with John was humiliating. Bob and I felt ashamed and degraded as we watched our boy line up to answer the court docket with the habitual town drunks. Rather than hiring a lawyer, Bob decided to speak to the judge on John's behalf. Bob thought he was helping, but because he didn't require John to deal with the consequences of his behavior himself, he was actually standing in the way of John's recovery.

The judge was no help either. Dismissing the charge, he told John he was fortunate to have parents who were trying to bring him up right and that he felt sure John wouldn't make the same mistake again. He ended by fining John court costs of $25 and told him to walk the straight and narrow in the future. John spoke just two words in court that day: "Yes sir."

John's arrest and trial had been just one more scrape for him to squirm out of. Two days later, he called Angelo and bought the biggest bag of grass yet — to celebrate.

Chapter ❧ Four

We Began To See
How Really Bad It Was

But we still thought it was only a phase —
a behavior problem — and that this time, going to
college could solve it.

Midway through John's junior year, he discovered that one summer-school course would give him enough credits to graduate a year early. He responded emphatically: "I'm sick of high school! I'd love to go to college a year early!" He wrote the necessary letters, looked up college catalogs, asked his school principal to supply transcripts. We watched in astonished disbelief.

Amazingly, John's grades were still well above average, with an SAT score in the top 1% for that year. Susie got wind of John's prospects and launched a campaign for him to apply to her own college.

The subsequent flurry of activity was a great morale-booster for our family. Mike thought how great it would be to have John out of the house. Bob and I pictured nights of peaceful sleep, no stereo blaring, no late-night telephone calls.

John voiced his own thoughts at dinner. "It'll be really cool to go to college! I can do anything I want, and nobody will be there to say, 'John, I wish you wouldn't do that,' or 'John, be in on time,' or 'John, clean up your room.' No more hassles! I can hardly wait."

We other three exchanged glances. We could hardly wait ourselves.

So John was accepted to college at age seventeen. Our hopes soared. Susie couldn't stop talking about how glad she was that John was coming to Chambers. Focused on her pride and love for him, she forgot how unpleasant his behavior could be. Another "geographic cure" was in the offing.

At summer's end we took a two-week family vacation in a cottage at the seashore. From the start, the boys co-existed peacefully, fishing, surfing, and goofing around with Susie on the beach. Bob and I read, swam, walked the beach, and enjoyed relaxing on the porch. Life had taken a positive and happy turn.

Halfway through the second week, after a perfect beach day, John and Mike failed to appear when I called them to supper. I called again. We waited, and when they still hadn't come downstairs, I went up and opened the door of their room without knocking — something I ordinarily never did. "Did you boys hear me call you to supper?"

Mike, lounging on the far bed, looked up warily from his comic book. John, cross-legged on the near bed, looked up uneasily too, as well he might, because in front of him was the upside-down toilet-tank lid, full of marijuana. I could not have been more shocked if I'd found him cuddling a boa constrictor. He'd been picking out the seeds and putting them in a spice tin.

My rational mind shut down and emotion took over. "What the hell do you think you're doing?" I yelled. On blind impulse, I snatched up the tank lid, rushed with it to the adjoining bathroom, and flushed the marijuana away.

The boys were stunned. Mike stood up silently, backing away from the fury to come. John also sprang to his feet. Full grown, he was fearsome, his jaw set, his face contorted with hate. "You goddam bitch, that's seventy dollars' worth of pot you just wasted!" He loomed menacingly over me, at the brink of losing control, drawing back his fist. "Goddammit, I feel like killing you, you —"

My instinct for self-preservation suddenly revived. I grabbed the spice tin, ducked, and fled, clattering down the stairs in fear of my life, an enraged John hard on my heels. At the foot of the stairs I dodged out of his way. As Bob moved to grab him, I shouted desperately, "Let him go!"

John flung us roughly aside and plunged through the screen door, in the black fury so typical of his behavior during those dark days.

Even after Bob put his arms around me I continued to tremble uncontrollably.

"Honey, what happened?"

I didn't know what John might do. "Better see where he goes." We stood watching at the screen door as John charged angrily between the dunes and took off down the beach away from the house.

Susan grasped my hand tightly in her ice-cold one. "Mama, what is it?"

I took a deep breath to steady myself and told the tale.

"Thank God he didn't hurt you!" Bob said.

"Mama, you took a big risk. You're lucky he didn't do something really crazy."

Bob sighed. "Obviously John hasn't given up smoking pot after all."

"How much did he have?" asked Susie.

"He said it was seventy dollars' worth. The box of seeds is right here."

Susie poured them into her palm — half a handful, like tiny peppercorns. "He had a lot of pot. He's either selling it, or smoking huge amounts."

As we sat there in a troubled silence, Mike came downstairs and went into the dining room without a word. Dinner had grown cold on the table, but he sat down and started to pile food on his plate.

"I'm so scared about John!" Susan said. "This is serious! Daddy, can't you do something about him?" Bob and I had no answers. "I'm serious! I think John's been doing an awful lot more drugs than you and Mama know. I love John, and if you let him keep on like this, something terrible will happen!" Her pent-up tears poured forth at last.

We could no longer escape knowing that John was in deep trouble. We were barely beginning to face up to the monstrous reality that his problems might be centered on drugs. What to do about it was another matter.

"I know you're right, Susie," said Bob. "We'll talk things over and come to some decision. But we certainly can't do anything right now. Let's try not to let it ruin our whole vacation. Okay?"

"Okay," said Susie through her tears.

Mike sat cleaning his plate in silence.

"Michael, why didn't you tell us John had all that dope?" Bob demanded.

Mike shrugged indifferently. "I didn't feel like getting killed."

"Come on in the dining room, honey," Bob urged me. "We don't have to let this business ruin everything."

"I don't believe I can eat right now. You all go ahead. I think I'll walk down to the dock before the sun goes down."

Frightened and sad, I was homing toward a place of serenity — the tidal marsh. The sun's last beams radiated over the expanse of watery grass. As I walked toward the dock, I prayed for comfort, just putting one foot in front of the other. God help me, I prayed, my heart leaden in my chest. Why was this happening to me? What had I done to deserve it?

Heartbroken, I wept, mourning the loss of my loving son. I feared and even hated the violent, unpredictable stranger who had taken his place. Why? I asked again through my tears. Why me?

I sat there on the dock for a long time, numb. After a while I could feel the salt breeze fresh on my face again and noticed a splash as a mullet jumped in the channel. Panic and despair were fading. As I watched the white egrets planing westward in the afterglow, my courage and inner strength came cautiously inching back. I didn't know what lay ahead; yet the peace that enveloped me at that moment was very dear.

At the cottage, Bob and the two young folks had finished supper and cleaned up the kitchen. The atmosphere was noticeably lighter. John was still out. Susie and Mike decided to walk up to the fishing pier. After they left, Bob brought two cups of coffee into the living room and sat down beside me. The house was very still. "Well?" he said. "Where do we go from here?"

"You know as much as I do."

"While you were gone, I came up with a plan. See what you think of this. For a month, until John leaves for college, we'll keep him absolutely grounded. We won't let him leave the house without one of us along. We won't allow his friends to visit. It's the only way to be sure he doesn't get hold of any more dope. I think we may just be able to get him straightened out."

"It's worth a try. I don't know anything else to do."

We agreed not to reveal the plan until we were home, to avoid adding fuel to a volatile situation. That night Bob and I comforted each other as best we could, praying we had solved our problem, hoping to work things out.

Toward bedtime, John barged into the quiet living room like a roiling thunderhead and launched into a profane tirade. "Mom, you're lucky you didn't get hurt." His voice was nastily self-righteous. "I felt like killing you. I still do."

I listened in silence.

"You think you're so holy and good, but the truth is, you're a criminal, a common thief! You stole my pot, just stole it!" His voice grew louder as his rage built. "Where do you get off, thinking you're in charge of my life? Dad's just as bad as you. He takes up for you in everything. Why don't the two of you just get off my back? I can

29

handle my life just fine, if you two goddam stinking hypocrites will ever get the hell out of it!"

We took it coolly in the wake of our new resolve. He may have realized how wild he sounded or else sensed a change in our attitude, for during those last few days at the beach, he didn't leave or carry out any of his threats. We ignored his rudeness, his sullenness and hostility. Placing complete reliance upon Bob's plan, we believed we would soon be moving ahead.

We also believed, naively, that a month of living clean was all John needed to get straightened out. How ignorant we were about his disease — so ignorant we didn't even know it was a disease. We were barely beginning to get a look at our particular monster.

We would later hear other families talk about a drugging kid as "the elephant in the living room." Everyone knows the elephant is there, but everyone ignores it. There had been a pachyderm in our parlor for several years. We had caught glimpses of trunk or tail but pretended we hadn't seen. People outside the family had seen parts of our elephant, too, but no one had identified it for what it was. Now we had seen the whole enormous beast at close range — its trunk, tail, ears, body, and all four feet. John's elephant could no longer be ignored.

Yet we still did not know its name, or how to take hold of the elephant's rope to lead it away. Although we had felt its leathery hide and heard it trumpeting at full blast, in our ignorance we would tiptoe around the nameless beast for nearly three more years.

No matter how we tried to enjoy the rest of our vacation, we still felt wretched. John's "problem" colored everything a dull gray. The sun must have continued to sparkle on the sea, but Bob and I couldn't see it. Susan tried to keep things cheerful — an uphill fight. Mike and John spent the last few days sitting glumly on their surfboards fifty yards from shore. At night they read comic books or fished apathetically from the pier. Nobody had any fun.

Back home, the essentials of our plan fell into place. John accepted his house arrest more readily than we had expected. Perhaps he really wanted to break free of his habit and was grateful for our attempt to help. He came to meals and watched TV peaceably with the family. He stopped shutting himself up in his room. In that month we saw more of John than we had in three years, and he was fun to be with again. He helped with the dishes, carried out the trash, even got a haircut — whatever we asked him to do — in a docile and agreeable way. Believing our family affection and togetherness could pull him out of his hole, we welcomed John back and were happy together. For as long as it lasted, it felt like coming home,

During that drug-free month, John and I had two or three long talks. One day we carried a picnic lunch to the mountains nearby. We walked among the trees, admired the wildflowers, and took in the beauty of the woods. Uncharacteristically open, seeming younger than seventeen, he appeared vulnerable and a little sad as we ate our sandwiches among the toadstools and the ferns.

I told him gently that he appeared to have become dependent on pot, that his dad and I hoped this month of staying clean before college was the chance he needed to give it up for good. He appeared to be listening. I hoped he wanted to break free, and perhaps he did.

John left for college at last. We prayed that he would be stimulated intellectually, make worthy friends, be transformed from an aimless and hostile boy into a directed, outgoing, dynamic young man. A new world of possibilities was available to John, but he was not yet out of the woods. We would need a better map than the one we had if he was ever to make it through.

Chapter ↝ Five

We Got Physically And Emotionally Sick, And He Got Worse

We were afraid he would die if we stopped rescuing him.

Fraternity rush was one of the first events of the school year; John threw himself into it with abandon. Susan was soon getting feedback from her friends: "Say, Susie, your little brother really enjoyed the rush party last night! He was drunk as a skunk by eight o'clock!"

John didn't appreciate it when Susie took him to task. "Listen here, Susie! I left home to get everybody off my back. My social life is my business. Your social life is yours. I'm not bugging you, so you can stop bugging me!"

We waited for John's letters, but none came. Bob and I had no contact with him unless we called. I longed to know that our son was popular, happy, and doing well. Bob only said, "I hope the boy's decided once and for all to leave the drugs alone."

John's first grades arrived — three C's and two D's. "Are you doing your best, John?" I asked him when we called.

"As well as I intend to do. I don't plan to study twenty-four hours a day like Susie. I plan to have some fun!"

"We expect better than that," Bob spoke from the extension line.

"Well, you'll probably be disappointed."

Our Parents' Weekend visit to John was a disaster. The gentle, vulnerable boy who had told us goodbye a few weeks before was gone. The "old" John was back — scornful, moody, rude. John knew nothing of the planned weekend events. He didn't introduce us to his friends and accepted our offer of a steak dinner (washed down with a couple of beers) with a notable lack of grace.

While Bob went to pay for our meal, I hung back to ask the all-important question: "Son, have you stuck to your resolve to stay away from drugs?"

32

He eyed me distastefully. "Why don't you shut up?"

"Shhh!" I laid a hand on his arm. "People are listening."

He shook me off. "Quit shushing me, dammit! Why did you and Dad come down here, anyway? It was your idea to come, not mine. The school invited you. I didn't, and I didn't care whether you came to the stupid Parents' Weekend."

John's brutal words hurt so deeply that I could think of nothing to reply. It was as though he had twisted a knife in my heart. My surly, alienated boy turned his back and stalked out to join his dad.

Hoping to regain my composure, I went to the ladies' room and combed my hair and dabbed ineffectually at my make-up, but when I came out of the restaurant I was still blinded by my tears. My coordination was so impaired, I stumbled on the doorstep and fell. My stockings tore, and my left knee was bruised, skinned red and raw. I got up as best I could and limped out to the car, saying nothing.

Inside me, where my heart had been, there now seemed to be only a vast, echoing, hollow place — a space that should have been brimming over with my son's gratitude and love. Instead, that cavern of loneliness was dark, empty, and cold.

Bob, unaware of what had happened or been said, drove us back to the campus in a tense silence. My leg burned and hurt, my knee still bled. I mopped it with a tissue, making it hurt more. Tears ran down my cheeks to drop unheeded onto my new silk blouse. I hungered for a cozy corner where I could curl up like a child — someplace soft and comforting and warm. But there was no cozy corner that night for me.

Back at the dorm John said he had to go to his room for a few minutes. We sat down on a bench to wait.

"Anything wrong?" Bob asked, noticing my sadness.

"Are you enjoying Parents' Weekend? I'm certainly not."

"I'm not either. John's acted like a perfect jackass."

"Let's just head for home," I said. "I don't think I can stand to stay any longer."

"Fine with me. I'll be relieved to get out of here."

When John returned we told him our plans had changed.

"Sorry you can't stay," he said indifferently. "I guess I'll see you around Thanksgiving." He waved us casually out of the parking lot, as I choked back hot tears of disappointment and hurt.

We were as powerless as ever to exercise any control over our boy. After that weekend I found it more comfortable not to see John, not to know what he was doing, not even to hear from him. I hoped the misery would stay buried. Still, each time I brushed against that sore knee, the devastating memory rankled anew.

Things got worse between my husband and me. Our son's situation so depressed us that we had no energy left for our own relationship. I was angry with my son and angry with my husband for distancing himself from the problem. While my head throbbed and my gut ached, I couldn't recognize the anger at the root of it all. Being angry went against everything I'd ever been taught — turn the other cheek, forgive seventy-times-seven. Instead of letting that anger out, I unwittingly repressed and translated it into chronic depression, self-loathing, and barely veiled hostility toward my good man.

The effort I expended in numbing myself bore other dark fruit as well. In deadening myself to anger, disgust, contempt, and fear, I also gave up joy, excitement, anticipation, desire. Our marital relationship went downhill along with the rest of our family life.

Physically I was a mess. My blood pressure went up, requiring medication. I gained weight steadily, yet food no longer comforted me. I would have to find other ways to make it through each day.

When I slept poorly for several nights running, I got into the habit just before bedtime of filling the bathtub with comfortably warm water, locking the door, climbing in, and soaking until my fingertips shriveled. The relaxation that followed could usually be counted on for one night's good, needed rest.

As for Bob, haunted by fears for John's future, he was suffering from insomnia, disabling bouts of esophageal pain, and chronic stress. He asked himself the same questions daily: Was our son mentally ill, or was he a sociopath?

John's disease had robbed us all of the joy of living.

Thanksgiving that year was just one of a long string of family holidays colored by bewilderment, suspicion, anxiety, anger, and fear. Eventually I came to dread the thought of a holiday, any holiday at all. Each one had its own burden of family tensions, failed expectations, explosive reactions, and misery rather than joy. I came to hate the very sight of a turkey, or a holly wreath.

Before Christmas, Susie made a bid for help. She went to see the college dean to talk about John. Dean Smith offered to meet with Bob and me. We drove down on the last day before Christmas break.

"John's gotten off to a bad start," I told the dean. "His school-work and his attitude are bad, and we think he's smoking marijuana pretty heavily. We haven't found a way to turn him around, but if the college will back us, maybe we can."

"After Susan came in, I checked around, and your assessment seems to be pretty much on target. What would you like us to do?"

Bob spoke up. "In a few months John will be eighteen. We're through supporting him at that point unless he gets some help. Does the college have a counseling service?"

"We have several excellent psychologists. I can arrange for John to see one regularly."

"He'll try to get out of it," I said. "I know John. He'll worm his way out of any plan unless it has some very sharp teeth in it."

"I'll supply the teeth," said Bob. "I'll tell him here in Dean Smith's presence that unless he sees the counselor faithfully, we're cutting him loose. Can you support that, Dean Smith?"

"Yes indeed. I'll have John check with me once a week to let me know how he's doing." The plan seemed watertight. Dean Smith picked up the phone to call John in.

We had stumbled onto an extremely useful tool: conducting any critical confrontation in the presence of an influential and impartial third person, somebody with clout, somebody who could create discomfort and inconvenience for our son, if need be.

When John walked through the door and saw us his surprise was evident.

"Thanks for coming in, John," the dean said in a conciliatory way. "Please have a seat. Your folks have come in today to discuss what I believe are some legitimate concerns. I'll let them tell you about it."

Bob took the lead, speaking decisively. "Son, your mother and I are very disappointed in the start you've made here. Your grades are no good. Your attitude is unpleasant, and your behavior is embarrassing your sister. We think you're mixed up with marijuana again."

John said nothing, staring grimly ahead.

"Dean Smith has agreed to back us in a plan," Bob went on.

"You'll be eighteen in a couple of months."

John glared at his father, emotion showing in his glittering eyes, his flushed cheeks.

"Unless you accept help for your problem now, your mother and I intend to cut you loose altogether."

John listened stonily, a muscle flickering in his jaw.

"You'll have to support yourself, but on the other hand you can live any way you please, with no interference from us."

"Unless you do accept help, John," the dean put in, "the college will assume you're not willing to put forth the maximum effort. At that point we'll require you to withdraw from school."

John sat in silence for some moments, visibly containing his anger. "Well. It looks like you've got me backed in a corner."

"I wouldn't call it that," said Bob. "We see it as a choice. It's entirely up to you. Accept help and begin to make the most of school, or get out on your own."

"It's not a choice, it's an ultimatum. You've obviously got me where you want me."

Dean Smith spoke up. "We're all on the same team here, John. Your folks want to help you, I want to help you, the college wants to help you. All you have to do is accept that help."

"What do I have to do?"

"When you come back after Christmas I'll have an appointment lined up with one of the school psychologists. You'll see that person regularly and report to me weekly on your progress."

"What if I don't do it?"

"I'll let your parents know, and you'll have to leave school. It's pretty simple."

"Okay," said John tersely. "I don't see where I have any choice."

"If you go along with this plan I truly believe things are going to get better for you," said the dean.

"Can I go now?"

"Yes. Thanks again for coming in."

John walked out without a backward glance.

A major milestone had been passed. We had seen John control himself in the presence of someone who could exercise power over his situation. He had revealed himself as a superb manipulator. He realized Bob and I had reached our bottom line. He gauged Dean Smith's power and, because he wanted the Chambers College diploma, modified his behavior rather than indulging in a violent outburst.

Surprisingly, things seemed better after that. Susan's boyfriend

Dave came for Christmas, bringing an engagement ring. Dave was a fine young man, and he and Susie were very much in love. We gave them our blessing, celebrating with a bottle of champagne. Their plans to marry after Susie's graduation brightened our otherwise gloomy horizon.

Early in the new year we phoned to check on John's counseling efforts. He said he had seen the counselor, describing her as "beautiful and nice." I had hoped for someone ugly and tough.

"Did you report to Dean Smith?"

"I went by his office, but he was on the West Coast. I'm supposed to go back later this week."

The next week Dean Smith was away from campus again, and John's counselor was "as nice as she could be." After the third week we saw that our plan wasn't watertight after all. Ultimately the counselor asked John whether he wanted to stop using drugs, and he said no.

"In that case, I really can't help you," she said. "You might as well stop coming until you do want to quit."

This well-intentioned "helper" failed John by not referring him to a competent addictions counselor. And she failed Bob and me by not steering us to a competent family counselor and family group such as Al-Anon or Families Anonymous.

Her failure to do so, and Dean Smith's failure to follow through on our plan, cost us significantly in money and time. When we saw that our plan had bombed, John's tuition for the rest of the year had been paid. We were right back at Square One.

Remembering my brother's tragic, wasted life, I saw despairingly that John was headed down the identical slippery slope. More than once I was obsessing about this parallel while driving my car and had to brake sharply to keep from sliding into the ditch or veering onto the wrong side of the road. It was all I could do just to take the normal precautions of life.

That spring John went to every party within miles and kept open house in his room the rest of the time. He and his pals became interested in a rock band called the Grateful Dead. Grateful Dead fans are aptly called "Deadheads," for many are heavily into drugs. John started traveling far and wide to concerts with his Deadhead crew.

John's roommate moved out, fed up with the Dead-mania and

drug-centered life. Lance, another Deadhead, moved in. We never met Lance, but on the phone he sounded like John's clone — resentful, sullen, uncommunicative.

The end of the school year found us at an impasse. John's grades were poor, but not bad enough to flunk him out. Bob and I were torn between our desire to cut him loose and fear that he would end up in prison or dead. And so once again we protected John from the natural, painful consequences of his behavior. Rather than taking the tough-love stance that would help him to get well, we continued to support him in his drug-centered life.

Chapter → Six

Wedding Bells For Susie

We got the courage to demand that John get help.

Susan and Dave set their wedding date. Thinking about gowns, veils, and flowers made a welcome change from worry about John. During spring break, Dave came to wrap up the final details. He and Susie began their premarital counseling, met with the organist to choose the music, and bought their rings. Orange blossoms were in the air!

John and Mike were visibly pleased when Dave asked them to be in the wedding. Susan came to me later. "Mama, you know I love John and Mike. We really want them in our wedding, but I can't help worrying that John might mess it up. Will you talk to him?"

"Indeed I will. Daddy and I want your wedding to be the happiest day of your life."

I sought out John and got right to the point. "Son, Dave has done you and Mike an honor by asking you to be his groomsmen."

"Yeah, I know."

"There's more to it than just dressing up in fancy suits. Daddy and I expect you boys to give Dave all the help he needs, as well as making our guests feel welcome. If you'd rather not be bothered, tell Dave now that you're dropping out."

"If Dave wants me in the wedding, I'll be in the wedding."

"Maybe I'm not making myself clear, John. You'd better not do the least little thing that could ruin Susie's wedding."

He looked me straight in the eye. "I'll do what I'm supposed to. I want the wedding to be nice, too."

After Susie's graduation the wedding excitement set in in full force. Presents arrived. The phone rang constantly. I put Mike and John to work moving furniture and setting up tables to display the gifts. Bob had them cut grass, trim bushes, clean the terrace, wash down the porch chairs. They had little time for mischief.

After a particularly strenuous day Bob and I had gone to bed early when, at midnight, the door of our room opened softly and Susie whispered to me: "Mama, can you come here?"

"Can't it wait until morning?"

"I don't think so. You'd better come."

I got up wearily and followed her. "What's the matter?"

"You need to go downstairs to see about John. He's sitting in the dark all worked up, smoking a joint and getting high. He says he has to talk to you."

"I'm worn out. He'll just have to wait."

"Mama, he's all nervous and upset. He says he won't go to bed until you come."

The last thing I wanted was a chat with my son the pothead. But mother love, or martyrdom, won out. I walked into the smoke-filled family room where John sprawled defiantly on the sofa. He had on a pair of ragged jeans and a tie-dyed T-shirt, a dirty red bandanna around his head. His eyes were puffy and inflamed. The TV flickered in the corner. A burned-out "roach" lay in an ashtray; he was finishing a second one.

"You're high, aren't you, son?"

"I've got a buzz going."

"I don't want to talk to you tonight. I'll talk to you tomorrow when you're straight. Go to bed, John."

My own calmness surprised me. I was making progress, able to detach. No tears welled up, nor did the old pain in my gut kick in. I was breathing easily, without fear. I did not lecture John or blame him, did not accuse him or put him down. I simply accepted the reality I saw and stepped back from the problem, making no effort to "fix" or "rescue" my son. I had begun my own recovery from addictive family disease.

"I'm not going to bed," John declared, folding his arms. "I've got a lot of things to say, and I plan to say them now."

"I'll listen for an hour, then I'm going to bed. I need my rest."

Recognizing my own need and setting limits! More good signs!

"Okay." Belligerent, John was also close to tears. "This is about you and Dad, and me and my life."

"Well, go on."

"You won't let me be myself — making me go to college, making me go to church, making me get haircuts, staying on my case all the time."

40

After a long trembling drag on his joint his manner changed from accusing to scornful. "You came down to school and put on that preposterous scene with Dean Smith. You don't have any idea how ridiculous you looked!"

Finding no hook to hang on in this free-form outpouring, I just listened.

"Another thing is living here. You're always putting off jobs on me that you don't want to do. I feel like a slave and you're the rulers! I get all the dirty work and none of the rewards."

"You can move out any time you like."

Stating the choices and being willing to live with the results — where was this empowered "new me" coming from? Wherever it was coming from, I liked the way it felt.

"If I move out, you and Dad won't send me back to school."

"Plenty of kids work their way through."

He changed the subject abruptly "Anyway, your and Dad's attitude stinks. Most of the time I feel like hauling off and punching you both. You don't have any idea how much self-control it takes to keep me from doing it."

Did John know that his behavior frequently produced the same reaction in me?

This time I refused to feel guilty or inadequate. I knew that what he said was not true. I knew I had been a responsible and a good parent, that instead of a slave's existence he actually had a privileged life. John's power to control my thinking was fading away. Reality was setting in!

He went on and on. I listened until he'd unloaded most of his emotional poisons and begun to calm down. All I got out of our encounter was that John still had feelings. In spite of his bravado, he was really just a frightened little boy. Finally he gave up and went to bed; so did I.

Newly freed from my old hopelessness and despair, I lay awake until dawn, not weeping and worrying, but looking for new strengths. My body seemed to be coming back to life after a hundred-year sleep.

That wee-hours encounter with John served to renew my determination to persevere until I found the help that would free our boy from his self-inflicted prison. There had to be a way out of this mess for us all; I resolved to keep on searching until I found it.

In the morning I told Bob what had happened and that something I had seen in John had revived my hope. Weary Bob couldn't believe it. After he left for the office with the old beaten look on his face, I turned over for a few hours' fitful sleep. Finally at noon I got up, showered, and dressed. John was still in bed.

Yet another plan was taking shape in my mind. I opened the phone book to the Yellow Pages under "Drug Abuse & Addiction — Information & Treatment." There was just one listing: "Substance Abuse Center — Family and Individual Counseling." I dialed the number, noting familiar waves of anxiety in my innards.

"Substance Abuse Center," a pleasant voice answered.

"I believe my eighteen-year-old son has a serious problem with drugs. Could he get some help at your place?"

"Yes indeed. We have several excellent counselors."

"We may have trouble getting him to cooperate. He's already been in counseling once, and it didn't help. My husband and I can't just leave it there. We want to do everything we can to help him turn around."

"Can the two of you bring your son in for an interview? Our first opening is two weeks from today, at three in the afternoon."

"We'll be there. White is the name. Our son's name is John."

"We'll see you then, Mrs. White. And in the meantime, don't give up hope. I'm sure things will work out."

Susie overheard the conversation. "Great move, Mama! Maybe this will be what John needs, since the college counselor bombed out."

Mike was pessimistic. "John will just figure a way to get out of going, same as he always does."

When Bob came home he was encouraged to hear I had taken this step. We agreed to say nothing to John. It was important to keep him on an even keel until after the wedding.

On Susie's wedding day, the weather was perfect. The church was bright with flowers and glowing with candles. The music was by turns romantic and grand. Dave, John, and Mike made a tall, handsome trio in their cutaways and gray-striped pants; the bridesmaids looked a dream in flowered frocks with garden bouquets. Clearly, Susan was radiantly happy in her bouffant silk gown and lacy, trailing veil. Tears came to my eyes during the solemn ceremony, for all the young people looked so beautiful and so fine.

At the club reception the bride and groom cut the cake and fed each other gooey pieces. Susan threw her bouquet and her roommate Lisa caught it. But when Dave made ready to toss Susie's garter, John was nowhere to be found. The newlyweds changed to their traveling clothes, eager to make their getaway. Eventually the search was abandoned and the other groomsmen grabbed for the garter without John.

He was still missing when the couple drove happily away in a shower of rice. Everyone lingered in front of the club, gazing after the car with smiles — everyone but Bob and me. We wanted to know where the dickens John was. As we re-entered the building, he came sauntering out of the men's room, wearing the pothead's expressionless mask. He had been in the bathroom getting high.

"Susie and Dave are gone," Bob said brusquely. "Susie wanted to tell you goodbye, and you weren't there when Dave threw the garter."

"Sorry," said John with a shrug.

"John, sorry doesn't hack it any more."

"Bob, shhh! Not now," I said. "People are waiting to speak to us."

When we were home at last, Bob was ready to explode. "John!" he shouted upstairs as John disappeared into his room. "Get down here right now!" John came, still in his wedding clothes. We three sat down resignedly for what must have been the hundredth such talk.

"I'm laying down the law," said Bob. "You defeated our efforts to get help for you at college, but you won't block us any more. A week from today, you're going with your mother and me to the Substance Abuse Center downtown. You'll be seen there regularly the rest of the summer. That's the only condition under which you'll be allowed to live at home, or go back to college in the fall. Is that clear?"

"Yes sir." No one could read the thoughts behind that stone face.

"That's all. Go take off the suit, hang it up, and stay out of my sight for a while."

Our boy really had done the best he could. He had carried out his part well, before and during the wedding. After that one bizarre night, he had been pleasant and obliging to all, and Susie's wedding had gone off without a hitch. John had existed without his drugs just as long as he could bear their absence. Now it was up to Bob and me to forge ahead with our new plan.

Chapter Seven

Good Advice/Bad Advice

Nothing is more crazy-making than a counselor agreeing with the addict that you're "too hard on him."

The Substance Abuse Center's director, Glenn, listened attentively as Bob began our tale. John drummed his fingers, crossed and uncrossed his legs, jiggled a foot, stared into the distance, loudly sighed. When Bob reached the really painful parts of the story his emotional control broke. "Glenn, I love this boy so much, I care so damn much about him, it's killing me to watch him destroy himself!"

To my astonishment, sympathetic tears brimmed up in John's eyes and color rose to his cheeks. Unquestionably, John still had normal human feelings.

After hearing us out, Glenn outlined his recommendations. "John, I'd like you to meet regularly with Dr. Luther, our psychologist. Are you willing to cooperate?"

"I guess so," said John indifferently.

"Doctor and Mrs. White, I'd like you to come in regularly to see Elaine, a counselor on our staff. She and Dr. Luther will confer and relay progress reports. Is that agreeable?"

Already I was questioning why the family had to be split up like this. The set-up allowed too much room for missed communications and one-sided reports. However, before I could express my misgivings, Bob spoke up: "We'll do whatever you say." So I kept quiet, ignoring my doubts.

Glenn added, "We'll have John come in first for some testing. We try to rule out serious psychological problems before counseling begins."

More questions ran through my brain. Three automobile accidents, two arrests and court appearances, a year of probation, untold family conflicts, repeated episodes of drunkenness and other drug intoxication. How serious did it have to be?

But then a different tape began playing in my thoughts. *These are the experts,* it said. *You've placed yourself in their hands. You must follow their advice.*

Before we left the office John came up, predictably, with an obstacle to the plan. "Nobody's mentioned my summer job. How do you suggest I keep these appointments when I have to work every day?"

"Your health is far more important than anything else," Bob said. "If the boss won't let you keep your appointments, you'll have to quit. It's that simple." Hearing Bob's resolve, John gave in.

And so we started another long hot summer. To our surprise, John showed up for all his appointments. He liked Dr. Luther and said their sessions were going well. After he had been in counseling for a month, he came in one night stoned. Next morning he admitted being high. "Mom, I know you feel bad that I've had a slip. I feel bad too. I plan to talk about it with Dr. Luther this afternoon."

John's actual slip was in letting us find out. He had never stopped using pot, even smoking during breaks on the farm. Invariably high when he kept his appointments with Luther, he deceived Luther along with everyone else.

Elaine assured Bob and me that John was making progress; I saw none. I finally went to see Dr. Luther during one of John's appointment hours. Over the receptionist's objections I made my way straight to Dr. Luther's door, knocked, and walked in. John and Dr. Luther seemed taken aback, almost like guilty co-conspirators. Before my courage failed, I spoke out. "Doctor Luther, John's dad and I don't see much change in John. I'd appreciate hearing your evaluation of his progress at this point."

"John, would you mind waiting downstairs for a little while?" the gray-haired man requested smoothly. John left without comment; I took his vacant chair.

"I don't believe you have a thing to worry about," Dr. Luther said. "John's coming along all right. We don't see any cause for alarm."

"But what about his drug problem? I hope you know about his slip."

"Mrs. White, John is no different from his peers. Nearly all kids smoke a little grass and drink some beer. He's just trying out his independence, feeling his oats."

I had heard these words before. My stomach knotted, my throat felt tight. Was I crazy? Was I making a big deal out of nothing? Was my son perfectly normal? Why couldn't I trust

these people? Why couldn't I trust my son? If my boy was fine, something had to be dreadfully wrong with me. Was there no way out of the trap?

Terminally discouraged, I thanked the psychologist and left. John came home that evening wearing a triumphant grin. "Thanks for coming down to the center, Mom. You really helped me out. Now Dr. Luther understands what I have to go through, trying to live at home and satisfy you."

That same month, Phil Donahue's TV show featured teen-age graduates of an addictions treatment program, along with their grateful parents. All spoke frankly both of the misery alcohol/other drug dependency had caused in their lives and of the bright prospects opening up in their recovery. A toll-free phone number was shown at the program's end.

We still spoke of John's difficulties as "a problem with drugs." To me, an addict was somebody with needle tracks up the arms, a flophouse failure who would hold up a corner grocery for twenty bucks. John didn't fit that picture. But I was gradually learning that there might be other pictures that went by the name "addict."

Making that phone call was my first admission that addiction was a real possibility for my son. The person who took my call asked questions: Are there behavior problems? Does he have trouble getting along with other family members? Is he irritable and moody, prone to fits of violence and rage? Has he been in trouble with the law? To all these, I had to say *Yes.*

More questions: Is he having trouble in school? Has he dropped out? Have money or valuables disappeared? Has he run away? John had long been a behavior problem, but he had had no serious trouble in school, nor had he dropped out. He had never taken money or anything valuable at home. He had threatened to run away but never did. So to all these questions I answered, *No.*

Denial took over. I began to minimize the problem, telling the counselor I had only called for information, that our problem wasn't a major one, and we didn't need anything as drastic as inpatient treatment.

He had heard it all before. "All right, ma'am. But if things get worse, and they probably will, you know how to reach us."

Soon afterward I bought a book, *Toma Tells It Straight — With Love,* by a former undercover policeman who works to keep kids from getting caught up in drugs. Toma told it straighter than I wanted to hear.

He itemized signs of drug dependency: behavioral changes, isolation from the family, secretive new friends, hostility, rebelliousness, disrespect, callers who won't identify themselves, immaturity, lack of motivation, dropping grades, loss of interest in hobbies and activities, auto accidents, red and light-sensitive eyes, habitual use of eyedrops, mood swings, depression, loneliness, manic excitement and rages, vile and abusive language, habitual lying, suicide threats — and we had seen it all.

"Confront your kid as soon as possible," Toma said. "Every day you wait is going to cost him." We had confronted ours, twice.

"If a kid hasn't left [home] voluntarily when he's out of school or of age," Toma wrote, "it's probably because he's afraid to. He may realize that he hasn't anything going for him." Was this why John hadn't completely blocked our counseling plan, why he hadn't left home for good? "He may try to talk you into paying for his college . . . Don't do it . . . Don't do anything to help him continue living with drugs." If only Bob and I could have taken Toma at his word! In spite of the evidence, we still resisted the idea that our boy was an addict.

In our summary conference at the Substance Abuse Center, Elaine announced patronizingly that John's counseling was successful; there was no reason he shouldn't return to college. "Just try treating him more like an adult. You'll be surprised how well he responds."

Luther's parting advice was equally misguided and, for an addict, potentially fatal: "Just keep your drugs under control, son. It's when you drink too much or smoke too much grass that things get out of hand. Watch yourself, and you'll be fine." John was happy to shake the hand Luther extended, for it represented an alleged expert's permission to keep on raising hell.

We delivered John back to college. As he hauled his stereo equipment into the dorm and Bob and I followed with awkward loads of coathangers, John learned that Lance, his last roommate, had flunked out. Undisturbed by this news, he found somebody else — a clean-cut young man with a ready smile and a firm handshake. Relieved, we told our son goodbye and left for home. It had been a hectic, exhausting summer. We appreciated a return to domestic peace and quiet.

But now we had no trustworthy source of information about John. We could rarely reach him by phone; whenever we called, John was supposedly visiting in someone else's room. When we tried the numbers his roommate gave us, John wasn't there. And John never phoned us unless he wanted something — usually money.

We kept his allowance low — barely enough for haircuts, toilet articles, an occasional date, or a pizza. John did without the haircuts, toilet articles, dates, and pizzas and spent every cent on drinking and drugs. When his money ran out, a buddy would share his stash. Campus parties were plentiful, and free beer could always be found. So our attempt to control John's drug use by limiting funds failed.

When a pal dropped John off for Thanksgiving we were shocked at his appearance. His hair was long, ragged, and unclean. He sported dark glasses and a straw cowboy hat, with a raccoon tail hanging down in back. His wallet was on a chain, and his feet were crammed into cowboy boots. He came in carrying a full six-pack of beer and two cans left from another. He had drunk four beers on the hour-long drive home.

"Hi, Mom, Dad. Dad, can I borrow the car?"

"You just walked in the door. Why do you need the car?"

"Tomorrow's Thanksgiving. The stores will be closed. I need some beer for the weekend." (The addict has to make sure his supply won't run out.) Bob gave John the keys, not stopping to think that John would be driving impaired.

More questions whirled through my mind. Is John sick? Why would he go out of his way to look and act like a bum? Why is he drinking so much?

I was so ashamed of the way our son looked, I prayed that none of our friends would drop by during the coming holidays.

Were it not for John, I would have had a glittering holiday dress, silver slippers, and sparkling jewels at my ears. My imagination took flight: garlands of greens on the stairs, mistletoe in the hall, a fire on the hearth. It was gorgeous, glamorous, like something out of a play.

But we couldn't invite anyone over, for there was no telling what John might do. And so, knowing we couldn't reciprocate, I declined everyone else's invitations. Just stay home and hide out in my old sweats — that was the safest way to go.

Chapter Eight

The Wool Pulled Over Our Eyes — Again

Would it ever end?

John surprised us in one way, however. A compulsive personality, John pursues his current craze with a passion until it fades and the next one comes along. That Christmas it was tie-dyed T-shirts — a Deadhead trademark. He took over our kitchen with steaming vats of dye, saying the shirts were to be Christmas gifts for his friends. In the midst of the dyeing Mike sauntered in. "What's all this ugly mess?"

"They're tie-dyed T-shirts, asshole," replied John.

Mike's jaw tightened. He shouldered John roughly out of the way. "Watch who you're shoving, big boy."

"You watch it! If Mom wasn't standing here, I'd kick your butt." Mike was now several inches taller than John and his equal in weight.

"Boys, I don't like your language, and I'll thank you to act your age."

"John's acting his age — three," said Mike, bending over to look in the refrigerator. John shoved Mike from behind, banging his nose painfully against a shelf.

"Goddammit, John, I've had all I'm gonna take from you." Mike grabbed John's shirt; it ripped. John picked up a heavy skillet. The boiling dye was in peril.

"Knock it off this minute!" I screeched, shoving them apart.

John couldn't leave well enough alone. "Little Mikey has to have Mom take up for him."

"Get out of this kitchen, John," I ordered.

"I'll be glad to get out, as long as this asshole is in it." He gave Mike the high sign on his way out the door.

Mike slammed the refrigerator shut. "You see what a jerk he is. I hate his guts. Mom, why do you let him get away with that stuff? I'd have him put in a mental hospital. That's where he belongs."

"Just drop it, Mike. He'll be back at school soon."

"The sooner the better." Mike carried a handful of cold frankfurters out to the back porch, where he wolfed them down in a resentful silence.

Hot tears welled up in my eyes. Again, I felt degraded, helpless, totally out of control. Keeping so many volatile temperaments from exploding was an impossible job. All I could do was simply pray that the problem would go away.

Once things got quiet, I noticed that one of the tie-dyed shirts was very small, colored in pretty pastels. John came back into the kitchen after a bit, the pupils of his eyes very large and black.

"Who's this little shirt for?"

"A girl I know." It was John's first mention of a girl in years. My curiosity was aroused, but he kept his secret to himself.

We gradually heard more about the girl — Amy. John brought her home for a weekend. They arrived with Amy driving her nearly new, well-kept car. She was petite, friendly, an Earth-Mother brunette who nestled close to John's side whenever possible.

Amy fitted in with our family routine, offered to set the table, chatted in a relaxed way, helped with the dishes, and sat down with a book when nothing else was going on. But she really came to life in John's presence. They held hands, whispered, gazed into each other's eyes. Seeing John in the throes of infatuation was something altogether new.

Amy appeared to like John's dominating ways. She never expressed a preference of her own. "Whatever you want to do, John," was her standard response.

After the weekend Bob said, "Didn't you find Amy terribly passive? She reminded me of a marionette, with John working the strings."

Amy often came home with John after that, and she had a civilizing influence on him. We tried to forget the tormenting scenes of the past. Their activities fell into a pattern. John called the shots, and as long as Amy did as he said, things went smoothly. Their relationship worked only if John could play the tyrant and Amy the submissive slave.

"Son, I worry that you show so little consideration for your girl," I told him.

"You only see one side of it. When she's here, she acts like Miss Goody-Good, but at school she's always whining and nagging me."

"About what?"

"Every time I go over to Gary's, she calls up and starts bugging me. It really pisses me off, and I tell her so. That's just one example." What John didn't say was that Gary was his chief drug buddy. Amy hated the way John acted when he was drinking or drugging; her calls were attempts to control his use. John proved his independence by getting high twice as often and drinking all the more.

We later discovered what drew Amy to John. A member of her immediate family was alcoholic, and the expression she saw in John's eyes was the very one her beloved relative so often wore. Being with John was comfortable, familiar. It seemed like coming home.

Amy was drawn like a delicate little moth to the only flame she recognized as love — the craziness and emotional turmoil of addictive living. Her behavior was typical of someone who loves an addict. She felt guilty. She blamed herself for John's excesses. She believed John's condition was somehow her fault and that it was her responsibility to turn him around. She kept struggling in vain, seeking the right combination of controls.

And so Amy nagged, scolded, begged, pleaded, promised, gave in, clammed up, isolated herself, went running back, had hysterics, cried, and yelled — all in the hope of halting John's downhill slide. She sat by miserably as John got high, hoping her watchfulness would somehow protect him. She suffered his abuses, telling herself she deserved them. She went to Grateful Dead concerts and pretended to be happy while everybody got stoned. She drank with John, smoked dope with him, tripped on 'shrooms and acid, trying all the while to find a way to touch his soul.

None of it worked. Finally Amy took a gutsy step, announcing she was leaving college to study abroad. "Okay with me," said John, "if that's what she wants to do."

After Amy left, he came home and got another summer job. Bob and I exacted a promise of no more emotional firestorms. John assured us all would be cool. By now John knew how to get along with others when it suited his purposes. That summer he was agreeable, cheerful, and polite. He had just one disturbing habit: he would come home from work, mix himself a huge Bloody Mary, down it in five or ten minutes, and follow it immediately with a second one — all this before an evening out.

After finding a couple of dozen empty beer cans in our garbage bin we knew John was drinking a lot, but we were used to alcohol.

"All college kids drink beer," we rationalized. John did his other drugs away from home. We never saw any concrete evidence, nor could we ever tell that he was drunk or stoned.

He made it to work on time every day, did his job to the satisfaction of his boss, kept himself clean and tidy, even sported a neat haircut — in short, a functional alcoholic. From our point of view, things looked good. We conveniently managed to overlook his compulsive drinking.

At the dinner table one evening, John said in his most earnest manner, "Dad, I need a car."

"You had one, son, and you tore it up."

"I know. But I'm older now and more responsible. I need a car at school, and before fall term starts I'd like to go camping with my friends."

"Your driving record is no good. I've been paying exorbitant insurance premiums for three years."

"I know, Dad. But that was in the past. I've got to prove myself sometime."

"Let me think it over," said Bob. "I'll talk to the insurance people and see what it will cost me. I'll let you know what I decide."

"Okay, Dad. But think seriously, will you? This means more to me than anything in the world."

Ultimately Bob decided to do the generous thing. "Here's my offer, John. If you can come up with half the money, I'll match it. Maybe you'll take better care of your car if you have to put up your own cash."

"Gee, thanks, Dad! You can count on me this time for sure."

"We'll see. But there'll be no drinking and driving. That's a must."

"You can count on that, too." Thereafter John stashed his paychecks in the bank with miserly glee. Bob and I coasted along in blissful ignorance, thinking how well John was progressing. As his bank account grew, his plans for the camping trip also took shape. He and three friends planned to camp in a North Carolina wilderness area, he said, then drive directly back to college when fall term began. He even produced a list of names: his friend Gary, a boy named Lew, and a third called Thad. Not only had he written down first and last names, he had supplied phone numbers too. "I'll pick up Lew and drive to Thad's house in Waynesville. We'll leave the car there and backpack up to Mount Pisgah. If you need to find us, Thad's folks will know where we are."

"And you'll be at college in time for registration?"

"I'll call you when I get there, so you'll know I made it okay."

In August John tossed his checkbook triumphantly on our table. "Fifteen hundred dollars! That's what I've saved. Dad, if you match it, I'll have three thousand to buy my car!"

John and his dad drove all over town looking at used cars before settling on one. The day of departure eventually came. John had packed everything the night before, and at daylight he rolled out of the driveway in high spirits.

We didn't expect to hear from the campers for ten days or so. College registration came and went with no word from John. I tried to call; no one answered the dorm phone. After two days had passed we were seriously worried. This time a student answered when I called the dorm.

"May I speak to John White?"

"I'm sorry, there's no one here by that name."

"That's funny. Would you mind going down to Room 221 to see whether anybody has moved in?" I could hear the noisy comings and goings in the dorm as I waited, holding the phone.

"Hello? That room is empty. No one's living in it." School had then been in session for the best part of a week; registration was long past. At dinnertime I phoned the eating house where John was supposed to be washing dishes for extra cash. John's resident assistant happened to answer my call.

"Is John White there, please?"

"No ma'am, John didn't come back to school this year."

On the brink of tears, I somehow managed to control my voice. "Are you sure?"

"Yes ma'am. He was supposed to sign in with me to pick up his room key, but he never showed up."

It was the worst moment of my life. Vivid pictures whirled through my mind: search parties, helicopters, rescue teams. I could see John at the bottom of a gorge with a broken back, slowly starving, dying of dehydration, wondering why no help came.

I redoubled my efforts, dialing the phone with fingers like spaghetti. I called John's faculty advisor, the college dean, anybody and everybody. Nobody knew a thing. It was the bleakest hour I had ever known. "Oh, God help us!" I prayed.

Bob arrived from the office and quickly became as frightened as I. Neither of us could really think straight, but I had the names and numbers John had left. Bob stood by, caught up in his own anxiety, as I dialed the number for Thad's parents in Waynesville, fingers trembling, heart skipping beats.

A recorded voice spoke: "The number you have dialed has been temporarily disconnected." I must have misdialed. Try again! "The number you have d—" I hung up, near collapse.

I tried Gary's home number. It rang and rang until finally a man answered, sounding zonked-out and cross.

"Is this Gary's dad?"

"Yeah. Whaddya want?"

My voice shook. "I'm trying to locate my son John. He went camping a couple of weeks ago with Gary, and we haven't heard from him since. Do you know where they are?"

"Nope. Gary moved out last year to live at the beach. I never see the kid. We don't get along."

"Well, thanks all the same," I said. Lew's family was my last hope. My knees were shaking so much that I had to sit down, and Bob had to dial the number for me. A woman answered.

"Mrs. Grady?"

"Yes?"

"My name is Betsy White. You don't know me, but my son John is a friend of Lew's. We haven't heard from John in a couple of weeks, and we're very concerned. Did your boy go camping in North Carolina with John before Labor Day?"

Her answer floored me. "Well, they did go camping, but not in North Carolina. They went to Colorado to see the Grateful Dead."

"Colorado!" I exclaimed, in disbelief. It had taken me two hours to come up with this information; I must have aged twenty years.

Mrs. Grady had some questions of her own. "Perhaps you can help me as well. What do you know about these Deadheads? It's all Lew can talk about." She, too, sounded troubled, bewildered, sad.

"We don't know a lot about it. There's a lot of drug-taking at the concerts. Some youngsters do nothing but travel all over the country, following the Dead."

"It doesn't sound good, does it?"

"Not at all."

"Now you let us know if you hear from John," she told me kindly. "We'll be worried about you both until we know he's back." A stranger's compassion can be a very moving thing.

By the time I hung up, Bob's anxiety had turned to hurt, his fear to fury. John had lied to us, not once but often, and over a long period of time. We felt stunned and betrayed — especially Bob, who had been conned into putting up half the money for the car.

We were also angry that no one at the college had notified us of John's failure to check in. I called the dean. He alleged that students often changed plans at the last minute and failed to appear. He said he wasn't worried about John but would ask around to see what he could find out and let us know if he heard any news. After I gave him the other three names, I could tell he didn't think much of the crowd.

We had now come to realize that the chief bond among the Deadhead crew John was traveling with was drugs, particularly LSD and other hallucinogens. The reality was an ugly one. It's a wretched feeling to envision your child thousands of miles away, dropping acid for the trip that may fry his brain forever.

Eventually the hoped-for call came. John was nonchalant but defensive beneath a thin layer of cool.

"Thank God you're back, John," said Bob emotionally. "Do you have any idea how worried we've been?"

"I don't know why," John answered offhandedly. "You and Mom are so overprotective it makes me sick! I'm perfectly able to take care of myself, although you can't seem to get that through your heads."

I had picked up the extension phone. "Son, we hadn't the slightest idea where you were. We could never have found you. What really hurt, though, was your deceit! We trusted you, and you let us down."

"Come off it, Mom. I told you I was going camping, and I did. I just didn't say I was going to the Rocky Mountains instead of North Carolina. What's the difference?"

Bob ignored his superior tone. "John, you had us scared to death. All we could think of was that you were in trouble somewhere, and we had no idea where to look."

"You make me want to puke," said John, no longer troubling to be polite. "You always make such a big deal of everything. I just hope you two will finally decide to get off my back."

Bob's reply was surprisingly steady. "As long as your mother and I are responsible for your welfare, it's our duty to be concerned about you. I'm extremely disappointed in your behavior. You lied to us, deceived us, and took advantage of our good nature and trust. It will take a long time to rebuild that trust."

"You can go screw yourself. I'm hanging up," said John, leaving Bob and me feeling less angry than unutterably sad.

Chapter → Nine

Sick And Tired Of Being Sick And Tired

We were at our rope's end
and finally John surrendered, too.

John's junior year was a disaster. His new roommate, disgusted, soon pulled out. Living alone, John did as he pleased, with no one to object. Amy was not there to check up, nag, or berate him. We didn't know his friends, or whether he had any. We had never felt more out of touch.

Then he wrote to us, asking to go to Greece on a college-sponsored program. We could imagine him being caught with drugs in his luggage, disappearing forever into a foreign jail. When we ignored his letter, he called to push his scheme, declaring the trip meant more to him than anything else he had ever wanted to do. He had used the same line in working on Bob for a car.

After the Colorado trip we were not about to indulge John. We tried to cut off the discussion; he pressed on, adding that his friend Thad was going and the two of them wanted to travel together. This argument utterly hardened us against his plan, for two long-haired, ragtag Deadheads would be a magnet for every narcotics agent on the planet. When Bob told him flatly there wasn't the faintest possibility we would let him go, John slammed down the phone without saying goodbye.

In spite of our boy's histrionics, we stood our ground. We knew we had to stop being part of his addictive merry-go-round. We were also learning to stop rescuing him from the consequences of his disease.

With things at this tense impasse, my old college friend Sally Ann came through town. We went out to lunch and talked and laughed, catching up on missed years. "Are you working now?" I asked.

"I counsel families with drug problems," she said, "but I enjoy it so much, it seems more like play."

"How did you get into that?"

"My son is a recovering addict. For years, our family life was a nightmare. Once we got the help we needed, I resolved to help others with the same problem."

"How's your boy now?"

"He's been clean for a year and a half, and he's back in school."

"Gee, Sal, that's wonderful! I'd no idea you had had all this trouble." Words I had not intended to say came out. "You know, Bob and I have also had a hell of a time with our son John. We think drugs are at the bottom of it."

Sally Ann was neither pitying nor shocked. "Tell me about it."

I had needed to tell someone about all the pain and anger and fear for so long, it just came pouring out. Sally Ann nodded encouragingly, listened with a lively interest. An occasional comment let me know she'd been down this lonesome road herself. After I told of the Colorado trip and John's obsession with going to Greece, she set down her coffee cup and gazed directly into my eyes.

"Betsy, there's something very important you need to know."

"What's that?"

"Your son has a progressive and ultimately fatal disease."

I thought I hadn't heard her right. "Say that again?"

"John has a disease called chemical dependency." She spoke slowly, dropping each word into my consciousness like a stone into deep water. "This disease is fatal if it's not treated. John is very sick. It sounds like he's pretty far advanced. You and Bob must do something, and do it soon! Otherwise John will die, probably within a couple of years."

What a shocking thing to be told! It took my breath away, yet I still give thanks every day for Sally Ann and her courage. For in so telling me she saved John's life as surely as tossing out a life preserver in a stormy sea.

And she saved my life as well. Chronically depressed, worn down with the effort of trying to get through to John, feeling hopeless and helpless, withdrawing from life, I was seriously overweight, with high blood pressure, chronic digestive problems, insomnia, relentless headaches, and irregular heartbeat.

I had resigned myself to living only for other people's needs. I had long ago lost my capacity for joy.

57

"I want to get this exactly right. Will you say what you just said one more time? I'll have to tell Bob, and I want to get it straight."

"John has a disease called chemical dependency. It's a predictable, progressive disease, and if it's not arrested, it will kill him. If he doesn't get treatment, he may also kill somebody else, in a car wreck or other accident. Or he may accidentally overdose, or pass out and choke to death on his own vomit, or commit suicide out of shame and despair. Chemical dependency cannot be cured, but its progress can be stopped."

She paused to let me take this all in. "John probably will not ask for help on his own. It's up to you and Bob to get him there. Fortunately, his disease can be arrested, if you act in time."

Immediately I accepted Sally Ann's every word, resolved to follow whatever advice she gave. After all our attempts to get help, finally, with the ring of experience and truth, someone I knew and trusted had defined the real problem for me.

"What can we do? We've already tried everything."

"He needs to be hospitalized in an inpatient treatment program — not a psychiatric hospital, but a chemical-dependency program. You and Bob must see that he goes."

"I have no idea how to get him to do anything."

"First, get hold of a book called *I'll Quit Tomorrow,* by Vernon Johnson, just as soon as you can. After reading it you'll know a lot better what you can do."

I scribbled the title on a paper napkin.

"Next, pick up your telephone — today — and call this number in Minnesota. Ask how soon they can take John. It's one of the best treatment programs in the country." I wrote down that number too.

"If they agree to take him, use all the leverage you have to get him there. Remember, he's seriously ill. It's truly a question of life and death. Tell him that unless he accepts treatment, you won't send him back to college or allow him to live at home or support him, and make sure you mean it!

"Cancel his car insurance — sell the car if necessary. Enlist the help of every person who has the slightest bit of influence with him, and don't give up until you get him in that hospital. Start working on it today. Talk to the school

authorities, tell them what you're planning, and get their help. Enlist his girlfriend to help if you can."

I was scrambling to take in her every word.

"Use the element of surprise to your advantage. Keep your plans quiet until you're ready to move. If he gets wind of what you're doing, he'll try every way possible to get out of going. It will be hard, but just hold your ground. Don't back down! You can do it! You have to do it!"

I felt alive again, daring to hope things really could change. It was time to act! As we hugged goodbye, Sally Ann said, "Let me know how it goes. I'll be waiting to hear."

I couldn't wait to share with Bob what Sally Ann had said. He called the Minnesota hospital that same day and learned they could take John as soon as we could get him there. Like me, Bob was also ready to reclaim his parent role. Fresh hope had restored our courage and strength.

I found *I'll Quit Tomorrow* and plunged in. Vernon Johnson's description of the disease of chemical dependency precisely portrayed our boy. The book focused on a progression of crises as the hallmark of the disease. It defined intervention, a specific method by which the family is trained to break through the abuser's defenses and get to reality. It spelled out how a family can use the next crisis to persuade the chemically dependent one to accept help.

Bob read the book as soon as I had finished it and became all the more resolved to get John into the hospital soon. We were laying a solid foundation for successful action. We waited and watched, readying ourselves to move when the moment came.

A week after Sally Ann's visit, John called to say he was leaving for a Grateful Dead show more than a thousand miles away. I objected.

His voice was flat, unfeeling. "Hang it up, Mom. I've heard all your speeches before. I'm going."

"What if we need to reach you, son?"

"I'll be staying with Chris, in Syracuse. You can get me there."

"Chris who?"

"I can't remember his last name, but he's a Deadhead. Anybody there can tell you." Chris, in Syracuse! Either John didn't want us to find him, or drugs were fast destroying his mind.

No immediate course of action occurred to us after that. We could have asked the highway patrol to apprehend John, although we never thought of it. It's probably just as well, for in the end he was brought to help in a way we could never have contrived.

Sometimes, when we are finally pointed in the right direction but cannot go further, our Higher Power intervenes for us, despite ourselves, despite our fear.

After the weekend we phoned. Safely back at school, John again brought up the matter of Greece. He couldn't stop talking about it, couldn't accept the fact that we would not let him go. This conversation also ended abruptly, this time with the phone being hung up by Bob. The next day Bob wrote John a letter, laboring long over his composition to be sure he was not misunderstood.

Dear John,
Letting you go to Greece would be unwise in the extreme. You're tremendously vulnerable because of your drug-centered life-style. And as you have thoroughly deceived and blatantly disobeyed us on many occasions, your mother and I are not willing to under-write any new frolics. Please understand that we do love you very much, and our love and concern for you are the main factors in our decision to refuse.

With my love, Dad

This letter sent John into an unparalleled frenzy. He called Bob at the office, interrupting his schedule of patients, and shouted and abused him over the phone. Bob reiterated in a firm voice that we could not put John at such risk. John raged on, spouting obscenities, pouring out fiendish depths of hostility toward his dad. The tirade was cut short when Bob finally said, "Son, it's final. I'm sorry," and hung up.

Bob had known when he wrote the letter that John would indulge in a temper fit, but even he was not prepared for such a blast of vituperation. John's ragings sounded like those of a madman.

As for John himself, he was staggered by this event. He realized he had been completely out of control and sought out Dr. Callahan, a favorite professor, for support. That gracious man gave him most of his afternoon, listening patiently as John poured out his frustration and pain. He let John know he thought John's reaction was out of line while also indicating his concern and desire to help. It was probably Dr. Callahan who kept John from going right over the edge.

That evening John called Susan and also poured out his agitation to her, for more than an hour. The moment their conversation ended, she called us. "Mama, Daddy, I just got through talking to John. I got really scared listening to him. He sounds like he's about to go crazy. Something has changed. The way he was talking about the Grateful Dead, he sounded like a religious fanatic. That was only part of what he said. There was a lot about God and enlightenment, but none of it made any sense. I think you'd better go see about him just as soon as you can." Her voice caught in a sob. "Don't wait! Can you go tonight?"

On the extension phone, Bob was trying to understand. "All this just because I said he couldn't go to Greece? He must be in a mighty bad way. He sounded crazy when he called me today too."

I tried to reassure Susie. "Thanks for calling, honey. We're not going to sit back and do nothing. Try not to worry. We plan to try to get him into a hospital for drug treatment."

"I sure am glad to hear you say that. Just don't wait too long. I love my brother, and I'm scared to death for him."

We decided I was the one to go. Bob might seem too threatening, and John was usually more comfortable with me. I was ready to set out at once; Bob prevailed on me to wait until daybreak.

So far Mike had not been involved; now I asked his opinion. "Mike, I'm planning to drive to Chambers early in the morning to see John and try to get him into a hospital for treatment of his drug problem. What do you think?"

Mike's immediate, fervent answer brought tears to my eyes. "Go for it, Mom!" Mike cared too, even though he took great pains most of the time to conceal the fact. He recognized how sick John was and wanted him to get help.

By four in the morning I was on my way. I shared the road with a few truckers under the dark sky, but my chief companions on that unforgettable journey were my prayers. I asked God to make John's heart ready and give me the right words to say. As the coral streaks of dawn spread across the sky, I knew I was not alone in going to do what I had so long been afraid to do. A Higher Power upheld me, along with my family's loving concern.

I was the only one making the journey, but all of us were going.

As the darkness retreated, anxiety melted away. Now there was only confidence and faith. I was strangely unconcerned about the outcome, knowing all would be well.

I drove through the college gates as early-rising students made their way to class. A sunny fall day was unfolding, every yellow and scarlet leaf luminous against the sky. I found John's room and knocked on the door. Hearing no answer, I opened it and went in.

Daunting was hardly the word for the sight that greeted me. The floor was ankle-deep in dirty clothes, beer cans, ashtrays full of butts. A bong sat in the middle of the room, its spilt liquid soaking into the filthy rug. John was asleep in the top bunk in a greasy sleeping bag. His hair was lank and dirty, his face pasty, and he had a couple of days' stubble on his chin. The room was hung with Grateful Dead posters; a ragged American flag sagged from the ceiling. The nasty odor of pot, stale beer, dirty socks, cigarette ashes, and unwashed flesh nearly choked me. John opened his puffy eyes.

"Hello, son."

"Mom! What are you doing here? Turn around for a minute, will you, so I can get up." I did as he asked. "Okay, you can turn back around." He had hastily pulled on a pair of ragged jeans. "Now, what did you say you were doing here?"

I hadn't known what I would say, but the words came as a gift. "I thought you were in trouble, son. I came to see if I could help."

Apparently that was the message John needed to hear, for his eyes glimmered with tears, and he came over to give me a trembling but powerful hug.

Through a process I did not understand, a change had taken place in our boy. I would not have to do the whole job by myself.

He was participating, responding, helping! When we released each other I saw that he was too moved to speak.

"I thought I'd spend the day with you," I said, breaking the tension, "if that suits you. What classes do you have?"

"Let's see — I have a nine o'clock, and then I'm free."

"Fine! After your class, we'll get some breakfast, then do whatever you like. This is your day."

"Sounds good, Mom." John had regained his poise. "Why don't you go over to the Union and get yourself a cup of coffee? I'll come after class." He knew I wouldn't wait in that room!

"See you in a bit, then," I said, and closed the door behind me. The campus was waking up. Students made their way to the post office, the library, to class. I felt remarkably happy. The Student Union was buzzing with young folks' chatter. I sipped my coffee slowly, enjoying being surrounded by so much vitality.

Outside the window, the drifting autumn leaves recalled the

sadness we'd been living with and our fears for John's survival. At length I spotted my boy striding cheerfully along. However raunchy his clothes and grooming, the look on his face was a happy one. The Chinese have a saying — "When the pupil is ready, the teacher appears." Was John finally ready? When he reached my table he was still all smiles. "Hi, Mom."

"How was your class?"

"Oh, okay. I'm through for the day. We can do whatever you want."

"How about some breakfast for starters?"

"Sounds great, if you don't mind waiting. And, uh, Mom, I'm a little broke. Could you pay?"

I handed him a $5 bill without comment. John had just received his month's allowance; it was gone. He stoked up on eggs, bacon, several pieces of toast, juice, and milk, then flashed one of his most engaging smiles. "I'm ready if you are."

We walked along under the brilliant trees to the parking lot. On John's feet were the skeletal remains of tennis shoes — just rubber soles and laces. He had wrapped duct tape around the few remaining shreds to hold them on.

"Son, have you any other shoes?"

"Sorry, Mom, these are all I have. I had some good ones, but I can't find them." Shoes, jackets, sunglasses — so many of his belongings regularly disappeared.

"First, let's find you a decent pair of shoes. Then we can have lunch somewhere nice and decide what else to do."

John was agreeable. As we headed toward the city, he brought up the old topic again. "I blew my cool yesterday when I called Dad," he said. "I'm sorry about that. But going to Greece is really important to me. Will you talk to him and see if he'll change his mind?"

This was the opening I had been waiting for. I inhaled deeply and took the plunge. "John, it's not negotiable. Your problem makes it impossible." No reply, but no resistance either. "Frankly, son, I think you'll find most things impossible until you come to terms with your basic trouble." I had said it. I was ready for any consequences.

The suspense lasted only seconds. A calm and guileless expression came over his face. "Do you mean drugs?"

"Yes, son, I do." I crossed my fingers and prayed.

"What do you think I ought to do about it?"

Glory be! The battle was over. I contained my joy, fearful that any show of feeling might cost me the ground I had gained. "I came

63

here to propose a plan. Your dad and I want you to take medical leave from college and check yourself into a drug treatment program."

Still no resistance. I could scarcely believe it.

"Well, if you think that's what I need to do," he said, utterly humble, "I'm willing to go. But I don't know of a place."

"Dad has already made arrangements with a hospital in Minnesota. A friend of mine told me about it after her son went there. She says it's a wonderful place, and her boy has been clean now for over a year."

"How long would I have to stay?"

"The treatment program lasts a month. You'll only miss a few months of school. That's not much, considering the importance of this thing for the rest of your life. I know we can work out the details." We had reached a shopping mall. I pulled into a parking spot and waited.

"All right, Mom. I'll go."

My shoulders dropped; the breath streamed out of my lungs. What a burden lifted! John himself seemed relieved, even thankful. Obviously, he had been waiting for someone to get him over the hurdle he could not clear by himself. I laid my hand over his on the seat between us. He stared straight ahead, unwilling to risk a glance at me.

"Son, I'm proud of your courage. You've made the best decision of your life, and I don't believe you'll ever regret your choice."

In my mind the rest of that day is just a rosy haze. We bought the shoes, had lunch at a little Italian place, stopped by a drugstore for shampoo, razor blades, deodorant. Suddenly I felt extremely tired. My adrenalin had run out. Lack of sleep the night before and the day's strains were taking their toll. "You know, John, I'm really too tired to drive home today. I think I'll check into the college guest house and stay overnight."

"Fine, Mom. Could we go out to dinner together?"

"You choose the place."

A long and untroubled nap followed by a refreshing bath worked wonders. John met me just as dusk fell, and we set off for the city again in an altogether new frame of mind. The Mexican restaurant was crowded and cheerful. Across the table from me with candlelight reflecting on his face, John looked very handsome — a white shirt, his face freshly shaven, his hair shining. His excesses had not ruined his looks. And the expression of tranquility he wore was one I had despaired of ever seeing again.

"Mom, I'm glad you stayed," he said, almost shyly.

"I'm glad too. We deserve a little celebration. I haven't felt this happy for a long time."

John's next comment caught me by surprise. "I went around to see all my friends this afternoon and told them what I'm going to do."

"How did they react?"

"They were really glad to hear it. They congratulated me and said they were happy for me. A couple of girls hugged me. I guess they think I need to go."

If John had made his plans common knowledge, he evidently was truly committed. "I'll write Amy tonight. I know she'll be happy. She's been worried about me for a long time."

When I dropped John off we were both more at peace than we had been in years. My sleep that night was long, deep, and restorative.

Next morning we saw the dean. "We're here to request a medical leave for John," I said, "so that he can undergo treatment for his drug problem. He hopes to come back to school for spring quarter, if you agree."

"Splendid," said the dean. "He certainly has my permission to go." He stood up to shake John's hand. "Well, son, I wish you nothing but good. I hope this puts you where you need to be."

"I hope so too," said John.

"Will you leave immediately?"

"I don't want to lose my credits for this quarter. After exams I'll go home, then on to Minnesota."

"I'll be thinking about you," said the dean.

John walked me to the car and stood pensively watching as I drove through the front gate.

Chapter Ten

The Last Mile Seems The Longest

We got our son back.

After leaving the campus I pulled off the road at the first corner to find a pay phone. Bob's anxiety carried plainly across the miles. "Bad news or good?"

"John's agreed to go for treatment as soon as his exams are over. The college will give him medical leave."

"Thank God! Thank God! Did you have a hard time persuading him?"

"You can't imagine how easy it was. He was gentle as a lamb, appreciated my coming, listened to what I had to say. When I suggested going for treatment, he agreed on the spot. Don't ask me what brought about the change. I'm just accepting it gratefully. Apparently I showed up at the critical moment, when he was finally ready for help."

Bob couldn't contain his joy. "I just can't believe it! What a wonderful relief! I'll give Susie a call, and you can tell Mike when you get here."

On my way home I had ample time to reflect on John's amazing turnaround. Why now? All those times I had prayed so desperately for a change: "Dear God, please make John stop drinking. Help him to leave drugs alone. Change him. Change him. Change him."

That was it! Praying so hard for John to be transformed, I was blind to my own need to change! So long as I reacted with self-pity, anger, and resentment, my boy felt he had to fight me. When I surrendered to a new way of thinking, everything else, including John, changed in response. Entering his dormitory room, I had approached him for the first time without accusing or judging: "I thought you were in trouble, son. I came to see if I could help."

Our Higher Power requires our participation in bringing

about change. No matter how much I love another person, I cannot change that person. I can only change myself.

The next weeks were busy. We bought clothes for Minnesota, arranged plane tickets, read the literature the hospital sent. A staff counselor phoned us for help in accumulating a history and to prepare us for Family Week.

I had to make one more important call. "Sally Ann? It's Betsy."

"Tell me quick!"

"John's agreed to go."

"You did good, babe! It's not usually that simple. When does he leave?"

"In a few weeks, after exams."

"Too bad you couldn't put him on the plane the same day. It's a big risk, waiting. Any party could be his last, especially if he's doing acid or coke. The longer the delay, the more likely it is that he'll try to back out."

"He won't back out."

"Don't be overconfident. Remember, his drugs are his best friend, the thing that's been holding his life together. He'll be afraid that once the drugs are gone, there won't be anything left of John."

"What should we do?"

"Hang tough. Keep your hand in his back. Don't let him wriggle out of going. Don't even let him know you admit the possibility. You've come so far now, you have to make it all the way. Treatment means saving his life. Keep telling yourself that, and keep telling him, too."

"Thanks, Sal. I need the encouragement."

"One more thing — give him the number and have him phone the hospital himself. By doing that, he'll be taking some initiative for his recovery. When he talks to the counselor he'll sense their understanding and concern. He'll feel much better after that."

"I don't know what we would have done without you."

"Oh, I just happened to be in the right place at the right time. One day you can see that some other family gets the help they need. That's thanks enough for me."

John phoned the hospital willingly, then reported back. "I talked to a really nice guy out there named Sam. I felt totally comfortable talking to him about my problem. He's been through treatment, so he knew where I was coming from."

"Great! Well, all systems are go at this end. We've got your plane ticket and the winter clothes."

"Who's flying out there with me, you or Dad?"

"Nobody. You're going by yourself."

"Aren't you afraid I'll split?"

"I don't believe you'd let yourself and everybody else down. You'll do what you have to do."

A very real danger was that John would indulge in one last tremendous drug blow-out. His Deadhead friends were having a big Halloween party. We knew it was useless to try to persuade him to stay away. He partied until the sun came up, crashed, then slept until late afternoon.

By the time he finally made it home at ten-thirty at night, he was just about burned out. He had a couple of beers and several empties in the car with him, but he had not eaten all day and was flat broke. Too beat even to eat the bowl of soup I offered, he fell into bed and slept for fourteen hours straight. (Later, during Family Week, it came out that John took the last of fifty acid trips at that Halloween party.) Bob and I rested equally soundly, knowing our boy was home and the nightmare was coming to an end.

Physically and emotionally, John was a wreck. He was pale, perspiring, jittery, restless. He described strange sensations: feeling hot all over and then cold, being unable to tell whether he was hot or cold, and just feeling generally sick. His heavy marijuana use had left him with a persistent dry hack, periodic sharp chest pains, and a deeper cough productive of black phlegmy stuff.

In actuality, we were dealing with withdrawal symptoms. Discovering that food would alleviate his discomfort, I kept a ready supply of sugary snacks and treats and offered them whenever his distress intensified. A couple of toaster tarts or a glass of pineapple juice usually made him feel better.

With time on his hands, John often hung around whoever was available, wanting to talk. One day as he lingered in the kitchen I risked asking a big question. "What drugs have you used, son, besides pot? I'm sure they'll want to know at the hospital."

He shrugged. "You name it."

"Well, I know about pot. What about cocaine? Have you tried that? Have you ever taken LSD?"

He was getting edgy. "A couple of times."

"How many times?"

"I don't know. A few."

"Five times? Ten? More than ten?"

"Yeah, I guess so." He would say no more.

I was naive to expect John to level with me, for alcoholics and addicts always minimize or deny their use even in the face of irrefutable evidence. What family members may know about an addict's use is usually just the tip of the iceberg. If you know a little, there's probably ten times more to be known.

The afternoon before John left for Minnesota, I was doing his last load of laundry. He opened the dryer to check on my progress and let out a curse: "Goddammit, what have you done to my tie-dye shirts?" It was Hostile John again, but this time I stood my ground.

"Washed and dried them," I said staunchly. "If you don't like the way I'm doing it, get your butt in here and do it yourself." I marched out of the laundry room and slammed the door.

He sought me out shortly to apologize. "I'm sorry, Mom. I don't know what came over me. I appreciate your trying to help. I know I overreacted."

"Okay, John. I'll forget it this time."

I helped him carry the clean clothes to his room so we could begin to pack. Halfway through, he lay back on his bed and stared moodily at the ceiling. "I've changed my mind about the hospital. I don't think I'll go after all."

Thanks to Sally Ann, I was briskly unsympathetic. "You may feel that way right now, but those are just transitory feelings. Once you get there you'll feel much better."

Addicts are super-aware of the attitudes of those around them. John saw that I would not and could not be manipulated around this point. He got up and we went on packing.

The big day came. Bob told John goodbye and went off to work, leaving me to drive him to the airport in the rain. The drive seemed to take forever. Another eternity passed before boarding of his flight was announced. I asked John if he was afraid of the experience ahead. "No, I guess I'm just relieved. It's something I've been needing to do for a long time."

Waiting, we gazed out at the runway in a companionable silence. The day was grey and dreary, the clouds low. As John's plane taxied toward us from the end of the field, a radiant, unexpected shaft of sunshine penetrated the clouds, illuminating everything with a clean and purifying light. And then the clouds lowered again and all was gray.

Final boarding was called. John stood up and enfolded me in a bear hug, the twin of the one he'd given me when I showed up in his dorm. Eyes shining, he gazed earnestly into my face, strong hands gripping my shoulders. "You take care of yourself, Mom, you hear?"

I nodded, too full of emotion to reply. He picked up his bag and made his way through the gate. As he mounted the steps he turned for one final wave before disappearing inside the plane. Our boy was truly on his way.

Several hours later our phone rang. "Well, I made it!" He sounded almost jubilant, cheerful and relaxed. "They're having a blizzard here, but I managed all right. Everybody here is just as nice as can be. Don't worry about me. I'll be fine."

John had turned the biggest corner of his life, ready to be healed, accepting the main chance. He had gratefully placed his life in someone else's hands, after so many years of mismanagement and waste.

The next news came by postcard:

Dear Family,

Everything's going real well and looking nothing but optimistic. I'm doing fine. I'll tell you what's going on when you come for Family Week. This experience will be great for our relationships with each other, as well as my own relationship with myself. I love and miss you all. See you soon.

Much love, John

"I think John's going to make it," Mike observed with a grin. Later came phone calls, always cheerful, always encouraging. We could hardly believe the change in John's voice. The boy who at home had seemed sick, tentative, depressed, was now reclaiming his health and wholeness, giving all his energies to the task. It was glorious, wonderful, almost too good to be true. Sadly, many families never hear the beautiful words we heard as John began to recover. I just pray that somehow every family whose life is blighted by addiction may find a way to heal.

When we started making plans for Family Week, young Mike balked. "John's the druggie, not me! I don't see why I should have to spend my whole Christmas vacation in a hospital with a bunch of potheads! I'm not going!"

Again, I called on Sally Ann.

"Make him go," she said at once. "When we went for our son's Family Week, our daughter was the most important one there. She knew things about him that none of the rest of us knew. She made a critical difference. Just tell Mike he has to."

Every time I relapsed into victimhood, the sound of Sally Ann's voice got me back on track. I told Mike his input might be critical in helping to save John's life. He grumbled, but he gave in.

That night while setting the table for supper, I was about to put the spoon the dispose-all had chewed up at my own place, when the New Me took charge, walked across the kitchen, and dropped that deformed spoon with finality into the trash. Not even an abused mom should have to eat with a spoon like that! In small ways as well as large, I was calling a halt to my life as a doormat.

Susan wanted to know if she should join us for Family Week. In view of her new marriage we decided she need not go. I now see that decision as a mistake. It has taken Susan longer than the rest of us to understand all the ramifications of John's illness and its effects on our family life.

Everyone who has an opportunity should jump at the chance to participate in good family therapy, with counselors who really understand family dynamics and alcohol/other-drug addiction. (See Toby Rice Drews' book, Getting Them Sober, Volume 4, for a helpful checklist on what exactly to look for in a counselor.) Family Week was the best thing that ever happened to the three of us who took part.

As the plane skimmed over the snow-covered prairie on our way north, our excitement mounted. We took a cab straight to the hospital and found John in his room, asleep. He was pale but looked peaceful and healthy. Bob woke him gently. John seemed fearful of having to face us. Mike tried an invitation to put him at ease: "When you get home, John, you'll have to go skiing with me and my friends."

"Thanks for asking, but I don't think I can," John said. "You guys might be drinking and getting high, and I can't participate. I have to center my social life in other ways." We were impressed. After that statement John seemed more relaxed.

My husband had a question. "John, I know you have a problem with pot and other drugs. But you don't have an alcohol problem, do you?" Today it seems incredible that a physician could ask such a question. Bob had been taught almost nothing in medical school about chemical dependency. Like most physicians, he failed to recognize alcohol as America's number-one drug. John set the record straight.

"I'm a chemically dependent person, Dad. Marijuana is my drug of choice. Although I'm not physically addicted to it, I am addicted to the experience of getting high. If I give up pot and switch to alcohol, I'll just be changing my drug. A chemically dependent person can't use any mind-altering substances."

This was the beginning of our whole family's education in addiction. John spoke of his disease in such a serious way, we knew he had gained a deep understanding in only three weeks. His heart had been truly open, ready to be healed.

"I have to say goodbye for now," he said. "It's time for my meeting, but I'll see you tomorrow."

Bob and I hugged and kissed our boy, confident we all were going to make it together.

Chapter ⇢ Eleven

Learning To Live In Recovery

We all needed healing.

Once over the anxious hurdle of meeting John, we could relax and take full advantage of Family Week. The rules prohibited further direct contact with our son until we could be taught more effective communication skills. Glimpses of John at lectures and in the cafeteria reassured us; he was smiling and serene.

The five days of Family Week were full. A variety of topics was covered:

> An Overview of Chemical Dependency
> Family Response to the Illness
> Feelings and Defenses
> Spiritual Aspects of the Program
> Change
> Communications
> Self-Awareness
> What Happens After Treatment
> Going Home [a scary one!]
> What Does Recovery Mean?

Many of the counselors themselves were recovering folks. They shared their wisdom and experience with humor and understanding, in ways that really helped. We learned that chemical dependency is classified as a disease by the American Medical Association, can be described in medical and physiological terms, and has a definable onset and predictable outcome. Untreated, it is uniformly fatal.

Sally Ann had already spelled out some possible outcomes of the untreated disease. We now heard some additional ones:

> Fatal alcohol poisoning
> Death by fire

Permanent brain damage from chronic intoxication
or use of hallucinogens

Cardiac arrest

Fatal hemorrhaging from esophageal blood vessels

Death from delirium tremens (D.T.s) or alcoholic
seizures

Violent death linked to drug trafficking.

After hearing all that, we knew we had done the very best thing possible for John.

We learned that chemical dependency is a "feeling" disorder. Mind-altering chemicals distort the addict's emotional state, and in response to the addict's destructive behavior everyone else in the family conceals true feelings and suppresses unpleasant emotions. These buried emotions accumulate more and more power until, like a time bomb, they are ready to explode.

We learned that age is no obstacle to chemical dependency. For nearly six years we had told ourselves John was too young to have a serious alcohol or drug problem, yet he probably was addicted soon after he turned thirteen. Recent research indicates that adolescents become addicted far more quickly than adults. The state of alcoholism or drug addiction that takes thirty years to become full-blown in an adult may occur within months or weeks in a susceptible teen, particularly if cocaine or "crack" is the chemical involved.

The genetic factor weighs heavily in families like ours. Our lecturer asked for a show of hands by family members with one or more alcoholic or addicted relatives. We stared around in astonishment as nearly every person in the room raised a hand. Here was the visible evidence that alcoholism and drug addiction run in families. Not every child from a family in which addiction occurs will become an addict, but some probably will. Family history of addiction is a risk factor about which every young person should be told.

Bob and I counted up all the relatives we could think of who had a problem with alcohol. Over three generations we counted eighteen individuals with a past or present drinking problem, with several more questionables including those who for one reason or another abstain. Obviously, we both had a strong family history for addiction; John was the unfortunate one of our children who drew the genetic wild card.

Does it sound crazy that we were happy to be told our child had a lifelong, incurable, potentially fatal disease? Our happiness arose from the discovery that John was not a psychopath, not schizophrenic, not inherently vicious, and did not need to stay sick. He had chosen to get well, and we were there to back him up.

Furthermore, we now knew that we were not crazy, not bad parents, not worthless people, and certainly not beyond hope and help. No wonder Family Week felt good!

Denial was the cardinal attitude that underlay all our earlier responses. We learned why we had not been able to see that we were dealing with a primary disease instead of a symptom. Parents dealing with a child on a daily basis fail to perceive the gradual downhill slide, while others who see the youngster less frequently find it obvious.

The family is often misled by the user's periodic attempts to cut down or stop. John had always been extremely cautious about having anything to drink at home. Offered a beer or a glass of wine in our company, he often declined, or, if he did accept, rarely finished it. And he never did his other drugs where we could know. Many people in Middletown could have told us soon after it began that John had a problem with alcohol and other drugs. We couldn't see it for the world.

We learned why our social isolation had become entrenched. Families with an alcoholic/addicted child believe they should be able to solve their own problems; they also believe that no other family has such a problem. Every member of the family thinks she or he has somehow failed. Parents assume guilt for the child's behavior. Other children begin to exhibit emotional disturbances. Discipline in the home is inconsistent and varies with mood swings. Children think they must take sides. Sober children become angry with the chemically dependent one for causing the family so much stress and pain. Everyone struggles to keep the Big Secret from the rest of the world.

As a rescuer, I believed I had to manage John's behavior and keep him from using drugs: limit his spending money, check up on him, leave him out of family events, make excuses for his behavior or his absence, dispose of any chemicals found. It was my dad's and brother's story all over again.

All such manipulation is doomed to fail.

In Family Week I learned The Four C's, which I come back to again and again to keep my thinking straight.

I didn't <u>cause</u> John's addiction.

I can't <u>control</u> it.

I can't <u>cure</u> it.

I am learning to <u>cope</u>.

Chapter → Twelve

Taking It All Back Home

Fresh starts are scary!

As Family Week went on, we all gained new insights.

I saw that I could no longer protect and rescue John. I would have to detach, let go, and allow him to take responsibility for getting well. My main task hereafter would be to follow through in working a recovery program of my own.

Bob learned he had been suppressing feelings throughout his life. He learned to express his own feelings and needs, to listen lovingly as others expressed their feelings and needs, and to match up his intellect with the desires of his heart.

Mike learned to be honest about his own partying.

To young people, when the noun "party" turns into a verb — "to party" — it means just one thing: drinking and/or other drug use. Parents hoping to understand their children's behavior must be aware of this special meaning.

Mike also learned compassion for his brother as he came to understand John's disease. He, too, learned to deal with feelings. "I think it's a waste of time when people cry," he told our group counselor in one tense session.

"Mike, those tears and feelings are very important to the person who's crying," the counselor said. "Whatever is making someone sad is the kind of thing we're here to talk about. We have to work those feelings through. So the next time anyone cries, keep quiet and let them do it, okay? And if you feel like crying yourself, go ahead and let the tears come."

"Okay," Mike replied with a shrug. But in that group he himself never shed a tear.

✧   ✧   ✧

Some final details had to be dealt with before week's end. Bob, Mike, and I met with John's aftercare counselor to discuss our concerns about taking John back home: his tendency to con people, the chemically oriented college social life, his Deadhead attachments. We were all appropriately cautious about John's ability to stay sober and clean. He was not cured, but the counselor observed that he had given every indication of a sincere beginning. We hoped that in the coming weeks and months the strong family system would give him much of his needed support.

John's written aftercare contract included three support-group meetings per week, faithful reading of recovery literature, finding a recovery sponsor, and staying in touch with the hospital by phone. How were Bob and I to monitor John's adherence to this program?

"He knows what he has to do to keep his recovery working," the aftercare counselor said. "It's his responsibility and his choice. Just let him know you're behind him with loving support and encouragement, but don't try to work his program for him."

We heard one additional final caution. "Now don't expect too much too soon. It took your chemically dependent son a long time to get as sick as he was when he came here. It will take him a long time to get stable and well."

Bob and I had already resolved to have no alcohol around while John was living with us. Abstaining and declining to serve alcohol to our friends was a small price to pay, when we considered that John would have to abstain every single day for the rest of his life.

Chapter Thirteen

The Pieces Fall Into Place

We're in charge of efforts, not outcome.

The first serious test of John's sobriety, and of our ability to let go, soon arrived. John announced he planned to meet Amy, who had returned from her study abroad, and go with her and some others to an all-night Grateful Dead show. This was what we had most dreaded — his reentry into the Deadhead world.

Bob and I set some conditions. We asked John to have at least two sober, drug-free companions at the concert and to promise to leave his friends and find other accommodations if the pressure to use was too great. Amy had already told John that she too was giving up alcohol and other drugs to support him in his recovery. A second sober person would be along — Tom, a friend of John's from freshman year. Tom had left school to undergo treatment a year before and was maintaining a good recovery.

John agreed to these conditions. Even so, we didn't feel we could put much faith in what he said. We had been burned too many times. Broken promises, clever deceptions, and outright lies were hard to forget. Just as John was struggling to live into sobriety, we were struggling to live into our own new attitude.

"If our life is going to be different," my husband said, "we'll have to start learning to trust again. Remember that slogan we learned in Family Week? 'Let go and let God.'"

It was a very practical help. I repeated those five words many times after John drove off. I must have said "Let go!" to myself twenty times an hour — whenever the old panicky feelings struggled to take hold. I had to trust John to handle his own situation.

At noon the next day he was back, wearing a big grin of satisfaction. Amy, Tom, and John had been the only three among their friends without hangovers. Feeling great, they wanted to shout with the sheer joy of being alive. Amy stayed on with us for a few days, renewing her ties to John as he told of his experiences in treatment. She attended a family support-group meeting with Bob and me and found it helpful for her relationship with the "new" drug-free John.

John told us he had been thinking about his need for a sober, drug-free roommate when he returned to college. After he learned that Tom planned to go back at the same time, they agreed to team up. Everything to support and enhance John's recovery was there.

✦   ✦   ✦

One morning shortly before John left he sat down at the breakfast table and stared worriedly at his plate.

"Anything wrong, son?" Bob asked.

"A dream I had. It was really scary, and I don't know what it means."

"Tell us about it," I said.

"In this dream, I was standing on the seashore, watching the waves roll in. I felt almost hypnotized as I stood there looking out to sea. Soon I became aware of something strange on the horizon. At first I couldn't tell what it was. This thing gradually got closer as the waves brought it in to shore. After a while I realized it was an enormous pumpkin, riding the waves like a ship. I was amazed. I called it the Pumpkin Galleon. I couldn't stop staring at it.

"As I watched, it kept bobbing on the water, coming closer and closer, until finally one gigantic breaker tossed it right up to where I stood. It struck the shore with tremendous force and burst into pieces.

"I was horrified when I saw what was inside." His face mirrored his fear. "It was full of bodies, dead bodies! They were piled up in heaps, horrible, rotten and decaying.

"I felt sick. I was so afraid, the only thing I could think of was getting away. And that was the end of the dream. When I woke up, my heart was beating like crazy, and I was covered in sweat. What do you think it means?"

We thought about it for a bit. "What do you associate with a pumpkin?" I asked.

"Halloween."

"Okay. What happened at Halloween?"

"I went to a Deadhead party."

"What happened there?"

In an awe-struck voice, John said, "That was the last time I tripped on LSD."

"Yes? Now, who was inside the Pumpkin Galleon?"

"Dead people. The Dead. I see it all now. The wreck of the Pumpkin Galleon is what would have happened to me if I had stayed with the Deadheads and gone on doing what I was doing on Halloween. In one way it was neat and fantastic, like a fairy story, but the people inside had given up all control of their lives."

We had begun to think John's problems were over. Our "honeymoon" was short-lived. We discovered he had had his first "slip" that spring, using hallucinogenic mushrooms with some of his old party pals. He didn't enjoy the experience, for it reinforced everything he had been told about his disease. He *was* addicted and alcoholic. He could not handle mind-altering substances, then or ever.

When the truth came out, Bob and I were disappointed, but not nearly as much as we might have expected. John realized he had gotten cocky and wasn't working his recovery program as he should. And Bob and I had not taken seriously the long-term implications of John's disease.

The most positive thing we could say about John's "slip" was that we reacted without resentment, anger, or taking it as a personal affront. We saw his "slip" simply as a symptom of a lingering illness. We were no more angry than if we had had a diabetic child suffer an insulin reaction. It was a healthy change in our thinking.

However, we thought it wise for everyone's mental health to lay down some conditions for having John back home. We told him he was welcome so long as he did the things necessary for his recovery: attend support-group meetings regularly, work his program, accept fair feedback, and strive to be open and honest. Out of our own need for a predictable life, we asked him to be home every night by twelve.

John accepted our conditions. He went back to his recovery fellowship and latched on to the program with renewed commitment. He appreciated the wisdom he found among the old-timers — those with twenty and thirty years of sobriety. We never had to remind him about meetings again. He always went cheerfully and of his own accord.

John now began to talk about a drug-rehabilitation career. He volunteered to help in a local court-ordered program for teen-aged first offenders involved with alcohol and other drugs. In this way he could test his vocational interest and potential abilities in the field. As a recovering addict himself, John was a powerful force for good with these troubled teens. The group's facilitator told him he was gifted in the work and called on him to talk with young addicts who were resisting the idea of inpatient treatment. He was able to persuade them to accept the help they needed. His strength in his recovery grew day by day.

Eventually I knew I had to have an answer to a question that had long puzzled me. "Son, I've always wondered why you gave in so readily when I came to see you and proposed your going for treatment. What happened to make you change?"

"It's something personal. When I get home I'll write it out for you. I'd feel more comfortable telling you that way." John's own words tell about his turning point far better than mine could, and the chain of events associated with it go far beyond my power to understand. Here's what he wrote:

> I first tried LSD when I was fifteen years old and rapidly became enchanted with it. I loved just sitting back to enjoy the hallucinations. Sometimes the experiences were very beautiful, at other times very frightening. Usually they were just plain weird. I loved it all. It was a chemically induced fantasy world, which I much preferred to the painful realities of growing up and meeting life on its own terms.
>
> I became very good at using LSD — that is, I didn't let it shake me. Friends had bad experiences and shied away, but I came back for more. I learned that the only way to "control" it was to surrender, to go with the flow, rather than fighting it.
>
> My experiences using acid became more and more bizarre, profound, frightening, and ultimately, mystical.

I experienced what I perceived as visions of the divine. At times while tripping, I felt I was in touch with ultimate truths, seeing the unity and interconnectedness of all things. I began actively seeking that experience, which I believed was communion with God. The use of LSD had become sacramental for me. It was the ritual act around which my spiritual life revolved. Achieving communion with God as I understood Him, through the use of LSD, had become the focus of my life.

On a particular day when I took a strong dose of very pure acid, I let the resultant sensations roll over me, anticipating the familiar peak experience. It never came. When I reached the summit there was nothing there — no God, no visions, no voices, no thunder and lightning — nothing. Above all, there was no communion.

It was made apparent to me through God's silence that I was way off track. The unspoken message was clear: my drug use was destroying me. My spiritual quest had become perverted, and only through abstinence from all drugs would the communion be restored. At that moment I swore off all drugs forever.

My "forever" lasted just eighteen hours, and then I got stoned again. I did not yet possess the tools I would need to stay clean. But my attitude had turned around 180 degrees. I was willing and wanting to change. I had the desire to stop using drugs, and I had an inkling that I could not do it alone.

While Sally Ann was telling me how our family could find our way to wholeness, John was in touch with a powerful healing directive of his own. Neither of us knew about the other's epiphany, yet we were being simultaneously led to freedom. No wonder he had tears in his eyes ten days later when I showed up in his room and offered to help. Fully surrendered, he accepted our plan because he had been unmistakably called to healing but didn't know where it was to be found. All the pieces of the puzzle were in place at last.

Chapter = Fourteen

Our Whole Family Heals

Recovery isn't a goal, it's a journey.

Recovery is for everyone in the family — not just the addict. After John's return to college, Susie had her new life to live, Mike was just settling in at college himself, and Bob had his work. All the energy I had been focusing on John and his problem had to be rechannelled in healthier directions. Where to begin?

Throughout adulthood I had frequently been depressed. Bob wanted to help, but neither of us knew what to do. During one of my worst spells, three separate friends recommended a new psychotherapist in town. With Bob's encouragement, I met with her to discuss long-term therapy. After several exploratory sessions, we committed ourselves to doing the work.

Kate was an enormous support. She honored and understood me, accepted me unconditionally, and asked only that I share totally out of my thoughts and my dreams. She was the friend I had needed for so long. In addition to the "talking cure" and looking at my dreams, Kate also led me into some essential body work.

Negation of everything physical had long been one of my chief defenses. The accumulated physical and mental strains were an unsuspected but constant burden on my body. Kate helped me to see it was time to stop treating my physical self as an adversary and reclaim the vital body I remembered from childhood.

Learning to recognize and deal with those strains, I became far more comfortable day by day. I learned to banish a headache or a backache simply through relaxation and special breathing techniques. Even more important, the body work facilitated all other aspects of our therapeutic work.

One of the most helpful relaxation techniques I learned was the "progressive relaxation sequence." Anyone can quickly learn to do this; it is a wonderful stress-reliever.

In essence, progressive relaxation consists in starting with a half dozen slow, full inhalations followed by equally slow and full exhalations, then carrying on with this same relaxation breathing while alternately tensing and relaxing various parts of the body in sequence. You can begin at the feet and move upwards, or begin at the head and move down. In the chapter entitled "Learn to Relax" in Toby Rice Drews' book <u>Getting Them Sober, Volume One,</u> the technique is explained in detail.

After you practice this exercise daily for a month, preferably at the time of day when you are generally the most tense, you will feel more relaxed and comfortable than you could have ever imagined possible.

Only do the following if you feel comfortable doing so.

I found it most helpful to tape-record the directions myself, so that I could then lie on a mat or carpet on the floor with my eyes closed and listen to my recorded directions as though some other person were leading me through the exercise.

In recording the directions, experiment with the timing. I waited for at least three breathing cycles while holding the tensed position of each body part. Once you have released the tension, allow three more breathing cycles to fully experience the relaxation that follows. Allow time for at least two more breathing cycles before you move on to the next body part.

Don't hurry through it! Hurry and tension are two of the things we are trying to move beyond. Give yourself plenty of time. Remember, you are feeding much-needed oxygen to your bloodstream, your lungs, and all your body's cells. As you breathe the new air in and breathe the old air out, you are breathing out accumulated toxins collected by your body during a stressful day. You may want to envision the bright new energy coming in with the breath and "see" the dark cloud of stress and anxiety escaping when you exhale.

Before you begin the sequence, if you can, make certain you will not be disturbed for at least twenty minutes. Half an hour is even better. I took the phone off the hook and muffled it between two cushions. I turned down the volume on the answering machine so I didn't hear callers' voices. I shut the door to the room I used, and put a note on the *outside of the door saying I was not to be disturbed.*

Some people prefer to sit while doing this; others prefer to lie on a mat on the floor. Whichever way you choose, before you begin, remove and set aside your shoes, your belt, any constrictive undergarments, and heavy jewelry.

If you lie down, remember that the floor is always colder than anywhere else, so if you think you might be cold, you may want to turn up the heat, or use a soft throw or light blanket for cover.

At the end of the sequence, make time to remain in the same position, resting, continuing the relaxation breathing and appreciating the new sense of refreshment that you feel. When you feel ready to get up, your headache or backache may be gone, and your whole body will feel more at peace.

While working with Kate I came to believe that I also needed a mentor in the spiritual realm. Although Kate was a believing person herself, she acknowledged that this was not her area of expertise and encouraged me to find a second person to help. Eventually I found Father Matthew and asked him to become my spiritual director. He consented willingly. The two of them, along with my husband Bob, provided the encouragement and caring support I would need to do the personal work that lay ahead.

Many outside demands were being made on my time. Other parents with drinking and drugging teens had heard about our family's success and were hungry for help. Bob and I were more than willing to give it. Our parent-support group became a first priority. We invested considerable time and effort in sharing the hope that had meant so much to us.

After several months of meeting with these other suffering folks, it dawned on me I had a creative gift to share with these families and others like them. I resolved to write our family's story as a help to all parents who so much needed to heal. In order to find the time required, I resigned from my part-time job.

Kate and Father Matthew helped me get the undertaking off to a good start. Father Matthew recommended that I keep a certain order in my days: a regular time for getting up, a regular time for prayer and meditation, a time for work, a time for exercise, a time for recreation. He also suggested I keep a journal to stimulate my creative juices to flow.

I did exactly as he said. I set aside a half-hour every morning for meditation and prayer. I kept a journal. I sat down at the word processor and wrote for several hours each day. I bought a telephone answering machine so I wouldn't be interrupted. And all the while Bob and I continued in our parent-support group.

Walking was the exercise I chose, since it required only a pair of comfortable shoes. Gradually I worked up to a half-mile, a mile, then two. I began to enjoy my day's jaunt. As my physical activity increased, my depressive symptoms decreased. My breathing became easier. No longer did I walk with my eyes focused squarely on my feet. I enjoyed the cloud patterns, signs of the changing seasons, songs of the birds, meeting other walkers and friendly dogs. Walking became a pleasure instead of a chore.

In my morning quiet time, I usually began with a reading or a prayer, reflected on it quietly, and then just sat, inviting the quiet and calm. When distractions came, I learned not to struggle against them, and eventually they passed on by. At the end I was ready for the day in a new way — relaxed and alert, not supercharged with adrenalin as in the past, but grounded in a more profound peace.

As I wrote, I drew on a creative energy far greater than my own limited powers. At times the words came to me faster than I could type. I felt quietly joyous, knowing I was creating something that was truly my own.

No longer sluggish or depressed, I had more energy and needed far less sleep. I stopped smoking. "God is purifying you for something," Father Matthew said.

After a while I began to think of doing something about my obesity. I looked up a local chapter of a mutual-support group for people who ate compulsively. That meeting was the right place for me. The members welcomed me with genuine understanding. After such a long time concentrating on John's addiction, I was finally ready to admit the need for help with my own.

Whenever I was tempted to rationalize or minimize my overeating ways, a remark of Kate's often came back to me: "Remember, Betsy, there were no fat people in the concentration camps." It's simple: when you can't overeat, you don't get fat.

With the support of the overeaters' group, my walking program, and sensible meals, I began to shed a few pounds. Eventually new clothes became necessary. As I shopped, the dreariness of my old wardrobe made me laugh. For years I had worn black, navy, gray, hoping to blend into the background. How depressed I had been, and how long it had lasted! Now I craved brilliant blues, lively reds, throbbing purples. The life stirring on the inside had to find its way out.

As my energies grew and my body changed, I also admitted to myself that the marital relationship between Bob and me needed help. When we had learned what was wrong with John, we sought the best specialized help we could find. Why not seek the best help now for our own difficulties?

I told Bob I had been thinking we might consult a well-known clinic that specialized in sexual dysfunctions. He jumped at the suggestion. Surely it wasn't too late, if we both were willing to try. Our inquiry brought a positive response from the clinic. We were accepted into the program with a date set for our initial interview. Our therapy would extend over a period of two weeks. We were to fly to the city where the clinic was located, stay in a nearby hotel, and visit the clinic every day.

We were both excited and scared as our plane touched down. Those two weeks turned out to be the honeymoon we had never had, the idyllic vacation away from family cares that we'd often dreamed of but never realized.

Our therapists at the clinic were empathetic, intelligent, and competent. Great care was taken to maintain a professional relationship and absolute confidentiality. After initial psychological testing and history-taking, the basic building blocks of any good relationship were addressed — feelings and communications. We nodded knowingly. "We learned all about communications and feelings during Family Week at the hospital with our boy." But after working with the topic for a bit, we discovered we still lacked some of the necessary skills.

We had to learn to use "I language" — to say "I need . . ." or "I want . . ." when there was some issue to be resolved. It doesn't sound difficult; for us it was a colossal undertaking. We practiced using "I language" in the simplest of ways, every day:

"I'm feeling hungry and I'd like a snack. I need to know how you feel about that."

"I'd like to look in the shop windows across the street, which means we have to cross at this corner. I need to check that out with you."

It sounds silly, but our difficulty in carrying out these simple exchanges let us know we needed to learn.

We were taught various ways to negotiate conflicts. We were shown how, when our needs and wants differed, to decide whose need was greater. Always, the needs of our mutual relationship were kept paramount.

Our therapists then helped us to use these new skills in reclaiming our natural sexual desires. At the end of each clinic session, we were assigned a task to carry out in the privacy of our hotel room. All these tasks taken together constituted a graded and careful progression of physical togetherness, respecting the bounds of emotional comfort for us both. No step was taken until we both desired and assented to it fully. Throughout the process, we worked hard to honestly express our own wants and needs.

Responsibility — response-ability — was the goal. No longer shutting down our feelings, we regained the ability to respond to each other with warmth and tenderness, releasing much new creativity for us both.

During the second week as we lingered over a candlelight dinner, our young waitress said, "I hope you folks don't mind my asking, but have you just recently got married?"

We burst out laughing. "Twenty-five years ago," said Bob. "Why did you think we were newlyweds?"

"You were leaning across the table, talking to each other in such a romantic way and holding hands, I figured you had to be newlyweds. Old married people just don't act like that!"

We did feel like newlyweds. It must have been sticking out all over us. Strangers stared at us with fascination. *You look happy,* their expressions seemed to say, *and we'd like some of it too.*

Getting our marriage back on track was a benediction for the rest of the family. Susan could stop worrying about us. John had often wondered whether Bob and I might divorce; he was thankful to see there was no chance. The most surprising result of our marriage's healing had to do with Mike — self-sufficient Mike, who kept his feelings to himself, who couldn't let anyone know he cared. At eighteen, for the first time in his life, Mike was finally able to say "I love you." He still grins every time he says it, happy now to be a full-fledged member of the tribe.

One Final Word Of Hope And Encouragement

Have you ever felt helpless, hopeless, and powerless to change the behavior of someone dear to you? I know exactly how that feels. Many days in my own life, I feared the misery would never end. And there were other days when I was too afraid to try to bring about any change at all, even a healthy one.

Yet, in spite of my anxiety, my fears, and my discouragement, a wonderful thing happened. Through my friend Sally Ann, a Power greater than myself provided the all-important word of encouragement and hope which I so desperately needed. Hearing that word from the depths of my pain, I believed it and acted upon it, to the best of my ability. And right away things began to change for the better.

I discovered that I was not helpless where my own destiny was concerned, that I was not powerless over my own choices and attitudes, that there was hope, and that there were people in the world who could help me discover how to make that all-important difference in my life.

Now, I pass along this same word of encouragement and hope to you. You may be powerless over your loved one, but you are not powerless over yourself and your own fate. You do have a choice as to *how* you will live the rest of your life.

My prayer is that you may very soon come to know the un-dreamed-of blessings awaiting anyone who enters into the recovery life. How strange that we never enter upon this new way until utter despair drives us to do so!

Where do we find the courage to begin? Our courage comes from others who have traveled the path before us and returned to share their experiences with us. We see their shining faces and long for the same "things" they have found — serenity, balance, the ability to laugh, and a radiant peace in their hearts. Those experienced travelers will be there to walk every step of the way with you. They are waiting in any meeting of a recovery fellowship — one of the Twelve-Step groups that have become a well-known part of modern life. I hope that you will soon seek out the traveling companions and the fellowship that can make the recovery journey real for you. You only have to reach out and take hold of it for yourself. For surely if anyone deserves it, it's you!

And if you cannot yet do this for yourself — do it for your child. Your recovery will surely be a power of example for your whole family.

Epilogue

Everyone who hears this story always asks me the same two questions: "How is your son today?" and "How are things between you and your husband now?" Happily, the answer to both questions is, "Just great."

The events recounted in this book took place more than a decade ago. As I write this, John has been sober and drug-free for twelve years. Having earned his master's degree in professional counseling, he has helped many other folks who also suffer from his disease. He gave his permission for me to tell our story in this book, hoping that the telling might save other lives. Lately he has begun to reclaim some of the interests that were set aside when the drugs took over, particularly playing bluegrass banjo. On the West Coast where he now lives, he enjoys playing and singing regularly with a bluegrass band. He is married, though not to Amy, expects to enter medical school soon, and has a happy life.

Susan and Dave are happily married thirteen years and have two precious young sons. Susan practices law; Dave is a television producer. In their household, everybody talks about feelings and learns to handle them in productive ways. Their two boys are growing up confident and with terrific self-esteem.

Mike's progress was somewhat delayed by a bout of serious illness immediately after he finished college. He ultimately required a kidney transplant, with his sister Susie the donor. The transplant was successful, and Mike has now completed graduate school, has a darling wife, and a baby on the way.

A year ago Bob and I decided to leave Middletown to move closer to Susan and Dave, Mike and his wife, and our grandchildren. We had great fun building a rustic house in the mountains — "camp for grown-ups" is what I call it — where we now live contentedly beside a rushing waterfall. We are happier today than we could ever have thought possible.

Bob still practices medicine and enjoys home life. Although he has given up running, he now studies the violin and plays tennis in his spare time. I enjoy cooking for family get-togethers, writing, doing recovery workshops, and volunteering at a shelter for homeless folks. One of my greatest joys is phone calls and letters from all over the country with good news from families this book has helped.

At long last, all our holidays are happy ones. No longer dreading these reunions, we now consider our family get-togethers opportunities to further enhance our already rich lives.

Of course, we may have more hard times ahead, for life never guarantees us a bed of roses. If they come now, we know we have the coping skills to see us through, confident and serene. The old, frantic, panicky days are gone for good. For that and for so much else, we are so grateful.

We are truly blessed in the happy way our lives have turned out — in part through good fortune, in part through commitment and hard work, but ever and always grounded in the Holy One's abounding love. You probably won't be surprised, then, that our new home just naturally named itself. How could it be anything else but —

"Glory Be!"

Special Sections

➥ 20 Questions:
Are You An
Emotionally Abused Parent?

Do you:

1. House and feed a drinking/drugging young person while requiring nothing in return?

2. Endure inconsiderate or abusive behavior in the belief that you have no other choice?

3. Put up with a drinking/drugging young person's infantile dependency for fear he can't make it alone in the Big World, when the reality tells you otherwise?

4. Stay home, when you'd rather be elsewhere, in order to "watch" her, so you can make her behave?

5. Stay away from home to avoid scenes and hurt?

6. Provide an automobile and insurance for someone who's a terrible driving risk because you're afraid of losing that person's love?

7. Provide a key to your home so he can come and go at all hours, even when you're aware of his drinking/drug use and how his late hours are affecting his grades or job performance?

8. Make excuses to the school, the boss, relatives and friends?

9. Lose sleep, wondering where she is, or whether she's been in an accident?

10. Find yourself obsessed with his behavior, even when you're at work or out to have fun?

11. Get calls in the middle of the night from the police, the hospital, irate parents, or strangers who refuse to identify themselves?

12. Believe your child would be all right if it were not for her undesirable friends?

13. Cover his bad checks or pay off his debts?

14. Say nothing when valuables go missing, alcohol disappears from your home cabinet, or over-the-counter or prescription drugs vanish from your medicine chest?

15. Shield the abuser from all painful consequences of her behavior, such as jail, expulsion from school, or getting fired?

16. Nag, preach, plead, and cry, to no avail?

17. Live in constant fear of what might happen to him, or what he might do to you, your other children, or someone else?

18. Believe the destructive behavior must be all your fault or the fault of other family members?

19. Conceal unpleasant facts from other family members so they won't get even angrier at the one causing all the chaos?

20. Neglect your own health, emotional needs, appearance, recreation, or social life?

1 or more "Yes" answers =
   Your situation is indeed unhappy.

4-5 "Yes" responses =
   It's time to examine your life and think seriously about getting professional help.

The three lists that follow are simply successful solutions other families have found that can inspire you to find solutions of your own.

After you have reflected on them, go on to do only those things and follow only those suggestions that feel comfortable and safe for you and your family.

In other words, go with the customary conclusion of meetings of Al-Anon, Families Anonymous, Nar-Anon, and similar fellowships: "Take what you like and leave the rest."

➔ 20 Ways
That Families Became Able To Overcome Their Fears So They Could Get Needed Help For Their Loved Ones

1   Joe, thinking as an engineer, could only see his son's alcohol abuse as a moral failure until his physician brother explained that the boy's inborn lack of a certain enzyme made it impossible for him to metabolize alcohol safely. Once Joe understood his son's out-of-control behavior as the symptom of a biochemical disorder, he accepted the need for and found specialized help.

2   Dorothy, a babysitter, also has an addicted son. One day she was reading the children a book about Sylvester, a young donkey who finds a magic pebble. When Sylvester foolishly wishes he could be a rock, immediately he becomes a rock! But then when he wants to go back to being a donkey, he is unable to do so. His lonely parents search ceaselessly for him, and eventually their love, combined with the magic pebble, sets Sylvester free from his isolation for a joyful reunion with his family.

For Dorothy, the end of this story was a magic moment. Although her addicted son couldn't find the way to transformation by himself, she saw that her own decisive and loving action might be the thing that would pull him through.

3   Anne Marie desperately wanted to guide her addicted daughter to help, but she was afraid. And so she prayed, "Dear God, please take away my fear." After she continued to pray but her fear did not leave her, she changed her prayer: "Dear God, please be with me even in my fear. I trust you to lead me and guide me. I know you will be with me no matter which way I must go." Remembering that her Higher Power was there for her even in her fear was what she needed to get through.

4 Walter found several rocks of crack cocaine and a loaded pistol in his 14-year-old son's book bag. This was deadly serious — somebody was going to die unless he made a definitive move. That same day he turned the drugs and the pistol in to the police and made an appointment for himself and his son to be seen at an adolescent treatment facility.

5 Frank is a very methodical person. After months of agonizing over his out-of-control son, he sat down and made two lists: a) what would be likely to happen if he did nothing, and b) what the possibilities were if he went to an addictions counselor for specialized help. When he saw it all down in black and white, he realized he would be foolish to delay any longer.

6 Charlotte had been going to Al-Anon meetings for months, seeking help in her struggles with an alcoholic daughter. At a meeting she heard a slogan — "How important is it?" — and realized she had been worrying about the wrong things. The way her daughter dressed, the people she hung out with, her ugly attitude — they were only secondary to the real problem that was causing all this. The critically important thing was finding the help that would save her daughter's life. That slogan gave Charlotte courage to do what she needed to do.

7 Leo and Angela had been worrying for a very long time about their disrespectful, rebellious son. One night after watching a video entitled "Clean and Sober," they recognized the true cause of their son's unacceptable behavior and saw that treatment offered hope. When the boy was arrested, Leo and Angela asked the judge to sentence him to a treatment program instead of jail.

8 Evelyn's next-door neighbor had a beautiful daughter who was engaged to be married. A month before the wedding, the girl's fiancé failed to show up for a date. When she called his home to inquire about the delay, his brother told her the paramedics were just carrying her fiancé's body out of the house. He had died while sniffing cocaine. This horrible event convinced Evelyn she could no longer put off getting help for her own son, who was also a cocaine user. What gave her the courage to act? Knowing that so long as he continued to use, any hour might be his last.

9 Sylvia found a crack pipe under the seat of her car after her son had driven the car the night before. She kept thinking about how she could have been arrested for having such a thing in her possession. She made a phone call to the nearest adolescent treatment facility, then picked up her son from school and drove him straight there for a chemical-dependency evaluation. When he threatened to run away, she told him that unless he cooperated, she would go straight to the police, tell them who the crack pipe belonged to, and let him deal with whatever consequences might follow. He did not run away.

10 Dan and his wife Neeta asked themselves what was the worst thing that could happen if they told their 22-year-old daughter she had to accept help for her drinking problem or else move out. They concluded the worst thing she could do would be to refuse. Even in that case they would not lose anything, for the family game of denial would be over for good. When they confronted her, their daughter heard the resolve in their voices. Her response? "What took you so long?"

11 José was visiting a friend one night, and they watched the film "When A Man Loves A Woman." José saw that the woman in the film behaved exactly like his girlfriend. He had been considering asking her to marry him, but he realized that he couldn't marry her until her drinking problem was taken care of. The next day he told her of his decision. Loving José as she did, his girlfriend consulted an addictions counselor that same day on her own.

12 Conflicts over their son Josh's destructive behavior had caused David and Teresa to separate. During the holidays, Teresa left Josh with David, and went to stay at her brother's house. While she was there, her brother's son went into diabetic shock. Teresa's brother immediately called the rescue squad to transport the boy to the emergency room. After everything had calmed down and her nephew was on the mend, Teresa called David. "It's time we did something about Josh," she said. "I think he's just as sick as my brother's child, and he too needs medical help. I'm coming home to work with you on this. Josh's life is more important than any differences between us."

13 Tommy and Letitia were always in turmoil over their daughter Sue Ann, and their marriage was starting to go sour. On a particularly bad day, Letitia said, "Remember before you had your appendix out, Tommy? You walked around hurting every day for a month. After the operation, the pain of healing wasn't half as bad as the pain of the disease." Tommy didn't see what she was getting at until she said, "Try to imagine having your appendix out a millimeter at a time, instead of getting it over all at once. That's what we've been letting Sue Ann do to us. Let's find the help we need and get the worst pain over with, once and for all."

14 Whenever Cindy wants to learn about anything, she reads a book on the subject. Her 13-year-old son Matt was becoming a continual behavior problem, and after she found a pint of vodka in his room she went to the library and started to read the best books she could find about teens and alcohol. On the basis of what she learned, she understood that unless she acted, his problem would only get worse. She took Matt to the local community services teen clinic and got a family addiction counselor lined up who could help them make the needed changes.

15 Frances had an adult son still living at home who was drinking heavily. One night he came in drunk and, when she tried to reason with him, pointed a pistol at her head and pulled the trigger. Fortunately, the gun jammed. Shocked into action, the next day Frances went to a local addiction treatment center and signed up for their free family-educational series. Once she learned through counseling and support-group help that she could change her reactions to her son, she told him he had to either get help or get out. He accepted his need for help, and Frances continued seeing a family counselor. She regained her self-confidence and started taking care of herself and doing the right things to support her son in his recovery.

16 Jack worked for a company with a fine employee assistance program (EAP). After worrying about his teen-age sons for several months, Jack made an appointment at the EAP and went in to talk about his concerns. In less than a week, the EAP counselor had arranged an appointment for Jack with a person trained in intervention techniques. In less than a month Jack's eldest son was on his way to treatment, and the younger son had signed a behavioral contract. No one at the plant knew that Jack had gone for help until Jack told them what a great resource the EAP could be.

17 Lucinda, a single parent, had a teen-age son who was always in trouble with the law. On television she heard a catch phrase, "A mind is a terrible thing to waste." It suddenly struck Lucinda that a young person's life was also a terrible thing to waste. She called her friend Sarah, a faithful member of Families Anonymous. Sarah agreed to take Lucinda with her to weekly meetings. After a month in the program, Lucinda was ready to follow through with arranging an intervention for her son.

18 Donald's church sponsored an annual Alcohol-Drug Awareness Sunday. No one in the congregation knew how tormented Donald had been by his daughter Lisa's aimless, self-destructive way of life. Martha, the speaker that Sunday morning, was a mother who had been through it with her own child. At the coffee hour after the service, Donald waited for a private word with Martha. Over the weeks that followed, Martha helped Donald work out a plan and use the next crisis in Lisa's life to propel her to get help. It worked. Lisa has made a wonderful recovery.

19 Ruby knew that a very high percentage of Native Americans fall victim to alcoholism and other forms of addiction, but pride kept her from admitting such a thing had happened to her son John. Eventually he was arrested and jailed for driving under the influence. While John was in jail Ruby went to see the medicine man, who offered his support. When her son was released, Ruby told him she believed he needed two kinds of help: help from the medicine man and the sweat lodge, and a treatment program off the reservation. "If you do these things, you will be helping our people," she told him. John agreed to go. Today he's an addictions counselor helping other Native Americans turn their lives around.

20 Bill and his father Jim work for the same company. Young Bill was entrusted with taking the payroll deposit to the bank every week. Eventually cocaine got the best of him, and he began dipping into the deposit to support his habit. Jim overheard someone say shortages had been noticed, with Bill the prime suspect. Jim saw what he had to do. "Son, I know what's been going on," he said, "and I love you too much to stand by while you destroy yourself. Unless you get the help you need, I'll have no choice but to tell the boss about your problem." Bill went to the company's Employee Assistance Program on his own, admitted his need for help, and was signed into a treatment program within the week. He thanked his dad later on for caring enough to step in.

20 Ways
To Keep Your Partnership Alive While All "This Other Stuff" Is Going On

1 Marilyn made a list of reliable sitters, friends, and relatives to call on when she and Lou felt they had to get away from the turmoil at home. She then called on someone from this list at least once a week for an evening out, once a month for a night away. At times when she couldn't afford to pay, she arranged with a neighbor to exchange sitting services instead. At the times when Marilyn and Lou did get out for an adults-only dinner, they agreed to keep their conversation on subjects other than their children during that special time.

2 Juanita asked Fred to help her learn to use "I language." Every day she found some simple opportunity to improve family communications in this way. Here's the model Juanita used: "I feel ___ whenever ___ happens. What I need from you is ___."

For example: *"I feel left out when you watch football and don't talk to me. What I need from you is to invite me to sit beside you and answer whenever I make a remark."* Juanita respects Fred's right to a free choice, but 99 times out of 100 he chooses to meet her need. Fred has even begun to use the same "I language" himself.

3 A new driver's license photo made Cynthia fear she was turning into a frump. She resolved to have her hair done once a week, started doing her nails herself, and made a daily point of wearing pretty make-up. As she began to care more for herself, Wayne began to think of taking better care of himself. He started going to the gym and lost 15 pounds. Both Cynthia and Wayne rejoice that their self-esteem and their relationship have improved.

4 Loretta considered fun activities she and Boyd might enjoy doing together: dancing lessons, a foreign-language class, a hiking club? Boyd said he would like to join a line-dancing class. The two of them now have several new friends, get some easy exercise, and have a pleasant interest outside their worrisome home life.

5 Jeff, a massage therapist, was giving everybody else massages while his own body remained tense and tight. After he taught his wife Sue Ellen a few simple techniques, the two of them could exchange this healing kindness regularly.

6 Tom felt left out because his new wife Lisa focused so much attention on her chemically dependent son. Tom finally got up the courage to tell Lisa his feelings. She asked him to suggest one nice thing she could do every week to make him feel special. Tom said he would enjoy having her give him a manicure. Now it has become a special thing they do together. Next, Lisa got to thinking Tom might also want to do some special thing for her. Because she was usually the family cook, Lisa asked Tom to make dinner on the night of her weekly painting class. Tom was willing to try. Once he got started, he really enjoyed it and began to work out some special recipes of his own.

7 Martha was worried that her husband might be getting bored with their marriage. Remembering how exciting it was when they were dating, she asked Lyle to consider scheduling a regular "date" once a week. Lyle liked the idea. They started off with a picnic-for-two by a beautiful lake in the mountains and came home feeling peaceful and restored. Martha and Lyle's regular date is now a cherished custom with them. They may just go window-shopping, take in a movie, or go for a drive by the shore. Whatever they do, it's their special time to reclaim the romance in their lives.

8 Lucinda and Kevin decided to get married. Kevin had raised an alcoholic son and Lucinda's daughter was an addict. When they bought a new house, Lucinda was pleased that the master bath included a garden tub. One day, after her daughter's rebellious behavior had made life in their household a real burden, Lucinda invited Kevin to join her late at night in a bubble bath. Even though Kevin felt silly at first, he soon discovered it was a very good thing for them to do.

9 Walter wanted his wife Mary to know how important their new marriage was to him, in spite of anxieties centered on Mary's addicted son. He chose an ordinary day on the calendar to bring home a small gift and a card telling Mary how much she meant to him.

10 Ruthie loves celebrations. She generally honors family birthdays by crowning the birthday person Queen or King for a Day and asking the royal one to choose how the day is to be observed. Last year, even though their older son was away in rehab, Ruthie announced plans for a family celebration in honor of her and Sid's 25th wedding anniversary. She asked each member of the family to prepare something special to share: a cake, a poem, a handmade gift. The son in rehab sent a loving anniversary card; the other children's contributions helped to let their parents know how much they cherished the marriage and the home.

11 Looking at herself in the mirror, Teresa saw that her make-up looked dated and old. She put on her best outfit and went to the mall for a complimentary make-up session, then bought the basic products recommended by the cosmetologist. When she walked in the house that night, her husband Leon said, "I don't know what you've done to yourself, but whatever it is, I sure like it."

12 Although Bobbie knew she needed to exercise, without a buddy to keep her on track, she found keeping a regular exercise schedule difficult. She asked her husband Tim what kind of exercise they might do together: walking, tennis, bicycling? Tim chose tennis, which they could play at their neighborhood park. When they invited the children to go along and have some lessons, the whole family developed a healthier life-style.

13 Rose, a writer, was wishing she could recapture the special feeling she had had when she first knew her husband Bob. She set out to write the story of their courtship, including everything that drew her to her future mate. She put in all the funny moments, the happy moments, the romantic moments. When it was complete, she made a book out of it and gave it to Bob as a special gift.

14 Steve likes to cook. On his wife Trudy's birthday, Steve prepared Trudy's favorite meal and served it to the whole family, telling them it was something especially nice he wanted to do for his wife and their mom. Trudy, to show Steve how much she cares, often leaves little love notes around the house: under his pillow, on the bathroom mirror, tucked inside his dinner napkin, inside his lunchbox. Finding one of Trudy's notes always gives Steve a special thrill.

15   Jerri and Topper needed some guidance with attitudes and actions that would support their own serenity and help their newly sober son. They decided to take turns going to a weekly meeting of Al-Anon or Families Anonymous. After her first meeting, Jerri came home really excited.

"People there understand what we've been going through," she told Topper. "There's no charge for the meeting, and you don't have to talk. You just go on in and let the program wash over you. It's great! At first, walking down the hall toward the meeting room, I heard people laughing and thought I was in the wrong place. I didn't see how anybody in our situation could laugh. After the meeting started, though, I knew it was definitely the right place. By the end of the meeting I was even laughing myself! Those people can help us learn a wonderful new way to live."

16   After her daughter began to attend A.A. meetings regularly and spend more and more time with sober new friends, Frances came to appreciate the "alone space" and "alone time" that happened when her daughter was out of the house. She told her partner James how she was feeling and helped him to see that occasional time alone was important to her. James thanked her for sharing her need and cheerfully honored her request whenever she let him know she needed some special time just for herself.

17   Tony and Marisa were exhausted from constantly having to stay home nights and weekends to keep watch over their teen-age kids. Somebody responsible certainly needed to be there, but finally Marisa realized there was no need for both parents to stay home all the time. She and Tony agreed to take turns having "time off." Each of them chose one night to take a break, with the other parent covering home base until the partner returned.

18   Dolores and Will were worn down with the inevitable routines in a household with several teen-age kids. Will had always enjoyed violin music and even tried to get the children to study the violin, but no one was interested. Finally Dolores said, "Will, you enjoy it so much, why don't you take the lessons yourself?"

Will scoffed. "I'm too old to learn something like that."

Jokingly, Dolores said, "Then I'm checking out. I don't want to be married to somebody who's too old to learn something new."

"Do you really think I could do it?" asked Will.

"Of course you can!" Dolores said.

Will mustered up his courage and started studying by the Suzuki method right along with the 4-year-olds. After a few years he was able to play with an adult chamber ensemble and loved every minute of it, even the hours of practice. Finding something that fed his soul was the key to new pleasure in life.

After Will's success, Dolores began to think of things she had always wished she could do. Eventually she signed up for a ceramics class and discovered the same kind of satisfaction in making pottery of her own design.

19 Jo and Bill each had home responsibilities that they found very arduous and unpleasant. For Jo, it was balancing the family checkbook and paying the bills. Payments were always late, and the bank account was frequently overdrawn. For Bill, it was keeping up the maintenance schedule on the family car. Tires wore out and were not replaced, and wear and tear from inadequate maintenance was costing them big bucks.

Finally Bill hit on the idea of asking Jo if she would be willing to swap tasks. "I think I would enjoy the bookkeeping and balancing the checkbook," he said, and Jo found that the car maintenance schedule was easy for her to keep up. From then on, they looked for more tasks one or the other found tedious, in order to swap.

20 Federico and Luz heard about a Marriage Encounter weekend in their parish church and decided they had nothing to lose by taking part. When it was over, they agreed it was one of the best things they could ever have done for their marriage.

20 Ways
To Nurture Your Other Kids
Even Though The Troubled One
Continually Stirs Things Up

1 Rebecca sat down and listed some activities her children might enjoy doing with her: making cookies, going for a bike ride, reading a story — these were just some of the possibilities. She then asked each child to choose one and set aside a specific time for doing it. While they were involved in the activity, Rebecca made sure to give her full attention to the child who was with her.

2 After an important talk with her teen-age daughter that happened spontaneously while they were washing dishes together, Janie saw this as a great way to make quality time for her kids. Now Janie and her husband Larry schedule one parent and one child for every dishwashing session. Even though a dishwasher came with their house, they prefer not to use it, because so many of their best conversations take place during these set-aside times.

3 Wanting to show his kids how much he appreciates them, Wes came up with his "Star of the Week" award. The award can be for anything: being a great storyteller, a super bike-fixer, a creative deviser of games.

4 Ken was glad to discover that many card shops carry a line of greeting cards meant to build kids' self-esteem. He buys one for his son every week and mails it to him.

5 Lovella was interested in her family's history, but nobody could tell her much about it. She decided to ask each person in the present generation to write the story of his or her life, including words and pictures. After everybody's story was done, the family set aside one

Sunday evening to read their stories aloud. Afterwards Lovella helped the children put them all together into a special scrapbook, to celebrate their life as a family.

6 When the arguments over what TV show to watch got to be intolerable, Frank, a single parent, hit on the idea of a month without TV. So that it wouldn't feel like a punishment, he brought home some new games and joined his children in playing them after dinner when homework was done. When the month was over, nobody wanted the games to end, so they agreed to limit TV to one hour a night after homework and play games for the second hour.

7 When Herschel's other children thought they might have played a part in causing their brother Lee to become chemically dependent, Herschel looked for ways to point out the truth: middle son Lee's chemical dependency is based in genetics. Nothing anyone did or said caused Lee to become an alcoholic or an addict, and chemical dependency is no one's fault. Even today Herschel occasionally has to remind the children that one person's inappropriate behavior can cause another person to feel stress, but it cannot cause addiction. "Nobody can make another person become an addict," Herschel tells them.

8 Proud of having carried important responsibilities as a boy on the family farm, Adam saw that he could give his children similar growth opportunities even though they lived in town. With his guidance, his pre-teen son learned to change the oil and filter on the car, and his teen-age daughter learned to see that all the family's bills got paid by making out the checks for Adam to sign. When these tasks became a regular commitment on the teen-agers' part, they felt important to the family's well-being and had a great sense of personal accomplishment.

9 Recently separated from her alcoholic husband and frustrated with family difficulties, Miriam was desperate to find a family counselor. However, she wanted to be sure of the competency of any counselor she chose. While reading Toby Rice Drews' book *Getting Them Sober, Volume 4,* Miriam came across a special check list telling how to choose such a counselor. She shared this list with her teen-age children, who were eager to begin their own recovery from life in a family where addiction had ruled. After reading it, they all knew they were ready to begin.

10 Carrie's daughter had been begging Carrie to let her redecorate her room. Even though some of her ideas were different from Carrie's, Carrie first decided to let her child choose how to make her space feel personal and unique. The two of them then did the work together, painting the walls and sewing new curtains and a bedspread. Sharing their feelings as they did the work made it an extra-special time.

11 When unsupervised teen parties became a problem, Kathryn and Jim devoted Friday night to their kids and their kids' friends, scheduling activities they could supervise: going to a skating rink, taking in a ball game, or having Movie Night at home, with appropriate refreshments. After a film, Kathryn and Jim always encouraged discussion about it, allowing the kids to express their true opinions and feelings without dictating how they "should" feel. The kids felt valued and listened-to, and the parents were rewarded by more open communications.

12 Camille is helping her children to become better able to identify and talk about their feelings. She uses a standard question, "How did that make you feel?" in search of one-word answers: *confused, thankful, resentful, worried, angry, glad.* As all members of the household become more comfortable identifying and talking about feelings, they also learn more productive ways to channel those feelings into action. The result is a more honest and functional family life.

Camille is also careful to help her children learn about alcoholism and understand that their addicted sibling is probably not capable of sharing his feelings in a straight way because of the toxic chemicals working on his central nervous system. But she gives her non-addicted children permission to be straight about their feelings without guilt that their brother cannot participate in the same way.

13 When Gloria's son Jamil wanted a pair of $90 sport shoes she could not afford, she offered to contribute $30 if he could save the rest. Jamil had to decide how much he really wanted those shoes, and he felt proud when he finally saved up the money himself. After buying the shoes, he took much greater care of them than if Gloria had paid the whole cost. What's also terrific is that Gloria, a divorced parent, felt no guilt because she couldn't afford to give Jamil all he wanted, to "make up for" being a child of divorce. She showed her son that love and values were more important than giving money.

14   Betty Lee got tired of telling everybody to straighten up their rooms and pick up their clothes. Finally she announced that the next Saturday would be "Messy Day" — no one would have to make up his or her room or pick up any clothes. (She made it clear this was a one-day only event!) The children saw that their mom could still be flexible and playful, and the next day they pitched in willingly to make everything neat again.

15   After weeks of argument about the upcoming family vacation, Richard and Sarah tried a radical plan. They allowed their teen-age children to plan the family vacation and cooperate in arranging the details: budget, schedule, destination, etc. The children settled on a camping vacation and worked out a budget, decided where to go, made the necessary reservations, planned the meals, compiled lists of supplies and went shopping for them. When they found their budget inadequate for their plans, they got busy earning extra money by baby-sitting, washing cars, and cutting grass to make up the difference. The vacation turned out great, and the whole family felt proud that the kids had worked together in this way.

16   Herb, a personnel director, noticed that his second son had become aimless and withdrawn, while the older, drugging one got all the attention. Herb had often referred prospective employees for testing of their interests and aptitudes. Why not do the same thing for his boy? He arranged for the second son to be seen for aptitude and interest testing before entering high school. The results proved invaluable in helping the boy plot his academic and vocational course. He gained important self-knowledge, took pride in his strengths revealed by the testing, and learned of areas of weakness that he could work to improve.

17   Rowena sorted out all the photographs featuring each child in the family, then helped each child put all her or his pictures into a special album. While they arranged the pictures, they reminisced together about the special times each photo brought back.

18   Paul had been wanting to take a computer class, but his working hours were so long he couldn't find the time to go. His middle-school daughter offered to teach him on the computer she had been given for Christmas. Paul made a willing pupil, and his daughter was proud that she could share her skills.

19 Harry, a clergyman who did a great deal of personal counseling, often used the Myers-Briggs Personality Test in his work. Realizing that his frustration with his son might be explained by a difference in their personality types, he asked his son, wife, and two daughters to take the test. Family understanding bloomed when everyone saw how many different personality types were vying for supremacy under their roof. Thereafter Harry found it much easier to be patient and tried to treat his children with as much understanding as he did those who came to him for counseling.

20 A busy trauma surgeon, Lorenzo couldn't seem to find enough time to spend with his children, and they were growing up so fast! Eventually he settled for a special 10-minute visit with each child before that child went to sleep at night. They looked back together over the events of the day, focusing on what they could be grateful for in that one day. Those ten minutes came to be all-important to both parent and child.

*See the following pages
for support groups to call,
additional information sources,
and books and tapes that can
help you and your whole family
to heal.*

Support Groups and Information Sources

Most of the following "World Service" offices can supply telephone numbers and addresses for recovery-support groups in cities and countries throughout the world. You can also write for information, enclosing a self-addressed return envelope.

Family Support Groups

→ *Adult Children of Alcoholics World Service*
Post Office Box 3216
Torrance, California 90510 U.S.A.
Telephone U.S.A.   310/534-1815

→ *Al-Anon & Alateen Family Groups World Service*
Post Office Box 862, Midtown Station
New York, New York 10018-0862 U.S.A.
Telephone U.S.A.   212/254-7236 or 212/302-7240
Telephone Canada   800/443-4525

→ *Families Anonymous World Service*
Post Office Box 3475
Culver City, California 90231-3475 U.S.A.
Telephone U.S.A.   310/313-5800 or 800/736-9805
Telephone England   071/498-4680
Telephone Australia   03/803-4793

→ *Nar-Anon World Service*
Post Office Box 2562
Palos Verdes Peninsula, California 90274 U.S.A.
Telephone U.S.A.   310/547-5800

Support Groups for the Alcoholic/Addict

↪ *Alcoholics Anonymous General Service Office*
Post Office Box 459
New York, New York 10163 U.S.A.
Telephone U.S.A.   212/870-3400

↪ *Cocaine Anonymous World Service*
3740 Overland Avenue, Suite 3
Los Angeles, California 90034 U.S.A.
Telephone U.S.A.   310/559-5833
National referral line (listings for U.S.A.,
     Canada, & England)   800/347-8998
Telephone England (London)   171/284/1123
Telephone Canada:
     (Calgary)   403/229-5213 │ (Ottawa)   613/739-0509
     (Montreal) 514/932-5555 │ (Prince Rupert)   604/627-1362
     (Winnipeg) 204/586-3360 │

↪ *Narcotics Anonymous World Service*
Post Office Box 9999
Van Nuys, California 91409 U.S.A.
Telephone U.S.A.   818/773-9999

Additional Information Resources

↪ *Cocaine Hotline*
Telephone U.S.A.   800/COCAINE

↪ *National Clearinghouse for*
Alcohol and Drug Information
Box 2345
Rockville, Maryland 20847-2345 U.S.A.
Telephone U.S.A.   301/468-2600

↪ *National Council on Alcoholism*
and Drug Dependence
12 West 21st Street, 7th Floor
New York, New York 10010 U.S.A.
Telephone U.S.A.   212/206-6770

Talks and Workshops
Led by Betsy Tice White

Programs offered:

- Forming an effective community coalition to deal with addictions
- Parent recovery — new strategies
- The church as a catalyst for recovery

In offering these seminars and workshops, Betsy provides to families, churches, schools, groups, and communities practical help and encouragement for the problems associated with alcohol and other drugs.

For information, call or write to:

**Betsy White
Post Office Box 144
Marble Hill, GA 30148
Telephone 770/590-7311**

Please See
The Following Pages
For
Books, Tapes
And Videos
From
Recovery
Communications,
Inc.

(See other side of page for more material and ordering information.)

BOOKS

No. of Copies

TURNING YOUR TEEN AROUND .... $11.95 _____

➙ *FROM TOBY RICE DREWS:*

GETTING THEM SOBER, VOLUME 1 (the million-seller endorsed by "Dear Abby" and Dr. Norman Vincent Peale and Melody Beattie, author, *Codependent No More,* who says, "Toby's are the best books for families of alcoholics."

No. of Copies

GETTING THEM SOBER, VOLUME 1 .... $7.95 _____
GETTING THEM SOBER, VOLUME 2 .... $7.95 _____
GETTING THEM SOBER, VOLUME 3 .... $7.95 _____
GETTING THEM SOBER, VOLUME 4 .... $9.95 _____
GETTING YOUR CHILDREN SOBER .... $9.95 _____
GET RID OF ANXIETY AND STRESS .... $9.95 _____
SEX AND THE SOBER ALCOHOLIC .... $9.95 _____
LIGHT THIS DAY MEDITATIONS .... $9.95 _____

VIDEOCASSETTES

- "Getting Them Sober"
- "Detachment, Separations and Healings"
- "Getting Your Children Sober"

$35 each .... 2 for $59.00

AUDIOCASSETTES

- "Does marriage counseling work if one partner is still drinking?"
- "How to tell if it's really alcoholism"
- "How to know if it's hereditary in your family"
- "Surrounded: When your spouse and child(ren) are all addicted"
- "How to help a teenage alcoholic/addict"

$9.00 each

→ 8-AUDIOCASSETTE ALBUM:
"COUNSELING FOR FAMILIES OF ALCOHOLICS"

over 3½ hours of counseling help from Toby Rice Drews

Topics include:

- When you feel guilty/crazy/enraged when they continue to deny
- Why 'we put up with it' and why 'we keep going back' • Dryness vs. Sobriety • When you feel depressed because you can't leave
- Intervention — how to make them go to treatment • Adult children of alcoholics • How alcoholics can charm their helping professionals
- Much more.

Regularly $80 . . . . *Now* for readers of this book: $49.95

ORDERING INFORMATION

1. Circle the items you want, on both sides of this page.

2. Please fill out the information below.

3. Tear out and mail this filled-out entire page (with a check or money order) to:

> **Recovery**
> P.O. Box 19910
> Baltimore, Maryland 21211

4. PLEASE INCLUDE $6.50 FOR SHIPPING AND HANDLING.

PLEASE PRINT VERY CLEARLY.

Ship to:

Name

Street Address

City   State   Zip

Area Code and Phone

Look for this upcoming book, available Spring, 1997, in bookstores:

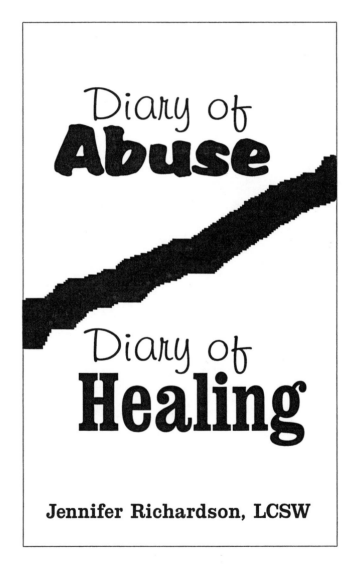

Diary of
Abuse

Diary of
Healing

Jennifer Richardson, LCSW